# Arts and Crafts

## Preschool/Kindergarten

The perfect arts-and-crafts idea right when you need it—that's what you'll get with *The Best of* The Mailbox® *Arts and Crafts*. The ideas and activities included were originally published in *The* Preschool *Mailbox* and *The* Kindergarten *Mailbox* magazines between August/September 1995 and June/July 1998.

www.themailbox.com

W9-BUH-208

**Editor:**
Karen A. Brudnak

**Artists:**
Cathy Spangler Bruce, Pam Crane, Teresa R. Davidson,
Susan Hodnett, Sheila Krill, Kimberly Richard, Rebecca Saunders,
Barry Slate, Donna K. Teal, Jennifer L. Tipton

**Cover Artist:**
Kimberly Richard

©1999 by THE EDUCATION CENTER, INC.
All rights reserved.
ISBN #1-56234-323-8

**Manufactured in the United States**
10 9 8 7 6 5 4 3

# Table of Contents

# Easy Art Tips

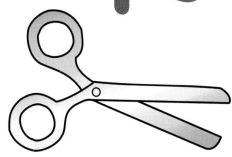

### Clever Clips

Do you have trouble displaying children's work on your classroom walls because of high humidity or tape that peels off the paint? Here's a solution: Hot-glue spring-type clothespins to the walls where you'd like to display children's work. Then simply clip the artwork to the clothespins. If you mount some clothespins at child height, youngsters can take responsibility for displaying their own work. Now that's a clever clip!

Kathy Lindsey—Gr. K
Waimea Elementary & Intermediate School
Kamuela, HI

### Get A Glue Clue

Clean empty nail-polish bottles and brushes with nail-polish remover. Rinse them in water and let them dry. Then fill the bottles with glue. As students use the brushes to apply glue to their projects, they'll be exercising their fine-motor skills. To keep brushes soft, periodically rub cooking oil on them. Good clue!

Kitty Moufarrege—Three-Year-Olds
Foothill Progressive Montessori School
La Canada, CA

### Finger-Fitting Scissors

Keep little fingers from slipping and sliding in too-large scissor handles with this helpful tip. Pad the handle's holes with a reusable adhesive such as Sticky-Tac. This material is pliable and can be easily molded again and again to fit different sets of tiny fingers.

Pat Davidson—Pre-K and Gr. K, Special Education
Padonia International School
Kingsville, MD

### Clean As A Whistle

Here's a tip that will help fingerpaint wash away easily. Rub a small amount of petroleum jelly on little hands prior to painting. Paint will clean right off!

Vail McCole—Pre-K
Tiger's Treehouse
Grand Junction, CO

### Handy Hang-Ups

Put an end to paint-smock clutter with this catchy idea. Affix the hook side of a long strip of Velcro® to a wall near your easel area. Attach a two-inch section of the Velcro's loop side to the collar of each smock. To hang up a smock, a child presses the Velcro on the collar to the strip on the wall. You'll have a neat and tidy art area!

Patricia Carpentier
Cedar Grove, WI

### Cleanup Kids Love

If an area of your classroom is littered with tiny paper scraps or glitter, loosely wrap a student helper's hand in masking tape, sticky side out. To clean up, the child repeatedly touches his wrapped hand to the littered area. For variety try wrapping the child's shoe in the same manner. Cleanup time is fun time!

Heather Peachey—Gr. K
Bowman School Extended Day Program
Lexington, MA

### It's The Bus!

While youngsters are still fascinated by the novelty of a school bus, use this idea to capture some fine-motor practice. To prepare, cut out a supply of white construction-paper squares and black construction-paper circles to resemble bus windows and wheels. Then mix a few drops of orange fingerpaint into yellow fingerpaint to achieve a school bus–yellow hue. Invite each youngster to paint a sheet of fingerpaint paper with the mixture. When the paint dries, use a marker to round the top corners of each paper so that the page resembles the body of a bus. Have each child cut away the corners, then glue on the window and wheel cutouts. When the glue is dry, encourage each child to draw faces in the windows to represent himself and his friends. Follow up this art activity with a rousing round of "The Wheels On The Bus."

Dorothy Jewell—Gr. K
Live Oak Elementary
Castaic, CA

### Here Are My Fingerprints

Each student's fingerprints will give this project a personal touch. In advance, copy the poem (shown) onto white paper; then photocopy a classroom supply. To make a fingerprint project, have each child write his name at the top of a 12" x 18" sheet of construction paper; then have him trace both hands on his paper. Instruct each child to press each finger (including thumbs) one at a time on a stamp pad, then onto the corresponding finger on each hand outline. Direct each student to glue a copy of the poem on his paper. To complete the project, write the date at the bottom of the paper. Here are my fingerprints!

Angie Mrowiec
Niles Park District
Niles, IL

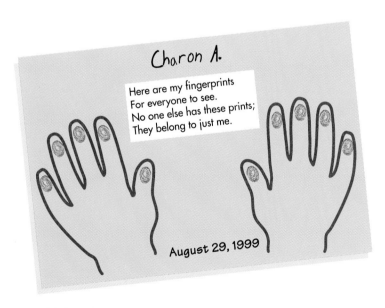

Charon A.

Here are my fingerprints
For everyone to see.
No one else has these prints;
They belong to just me.

August 29, 1999

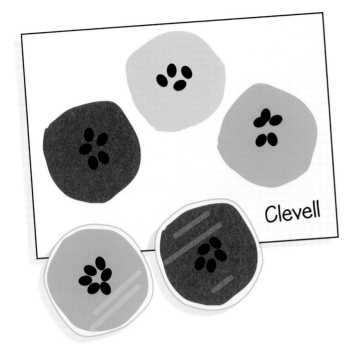

Clevell

## Apple Surprise

Leave youngsters starry-eyed when you cut several apples in half horizontally. Surprise! There are seedy stars inside! For a related art activity, pour green, red, yellow, and black tempera paint into separate pie tins. Cover a work area with newspaper. Personalize a white sheet of construction paper for each child. Provide each child an opportunity to dip an apple half into the red, yellow, or green paint, then press it onto his paper. After he has made several prints, instruct him to dip a finger in the black paint and then press it several times in the center of each apple print. When the paint is dry, display each set of prints or assist youngsters in cutting around the shape of each apple print. Laminate the cutouts if desired; then display them around a bulletin board for a delicious fall border.

Tammy Bruhn—Pre-K
Temperance, MI

## Apple Windsock

Breeze into a new year by making an apple windsock. To begin, glue red, yellow, and green apple cutouts onto a piece of fingerpaint paper. Add a number of similarly colored dot stickers. Cut crepe-paper streamers into varying lengths and attach them along the bottom edge of the paper. Bring the sides of the paper together and tape. On the top, punch four equally spaced holes; then attach string and suspend the windsock from the ceiling or under a covered play area. This versatile craft can be adapted to suit any topic or holiday season.

Rose Semmel
Stanton Learning Center
Stanton, NJ

### Hand-Picked Apples

Continue your back-to-school apple theme with this handy idea. Fill separate pie pans with red and green washable tempera paint. Spread brown washable tempera paint in a shallow baking sheet. To create a design that resembles a tree trunk and limbs, ask a child to press his forearm and hand in the brown paint, then onto a personalized 12" x 18" sheet of blue construction paper. Assist the child in cleaning his arm. Next direct him to dip his thumb into the green paint and then press it onto the paper to resemble leaves on the tree. Direct him to dip a finger in the red paint, then onto the tree to resemble apples. When each child has printed a tree and the paint is dry, display the trees together in a row. That's quite an orchard you have there. It must be time to gather the harvest!

Sedona O'Hara—Preschool
University Children's School
California, PA

### Stained-Glass Apples

The stained-glass effect of these apples is bright and beautiful. To begin, fold a piece of red, yellow, or green construction paper in half. Cut out a half-apple shape; then cut out the center of the apple as shown. Pour a generous amount of glue onto a sheet of waxed paper. Spread the glue over the paper using a paintbrush or fingers. Press red, yellow, and green tissue-paper squares over the glue, covering a space slightly larger than the apple cutout. Place the apple cutout onto the waxed paper and tissue squares, adding glue around the edge of the cutout as necessary. Dry overnight; then peel off the waxed paper.

Trim the excess tissue paper from around the apple shape. Consider laminating the apples as a finishing touch. Display the apples on windows for a look that will brighten your classroom.

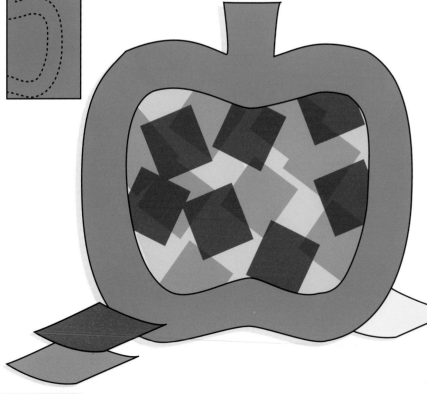

## See-Through Schoolhouse

These colorful schoolhouses will add a delightful touch to your classroom decor. For each child, duplicate the schoolhouse pattern (page 99) on construction paper; then cut it out. Using a craft knife, cut out the windows and door on each schoolhouse. Then have each child glue a piece of colored cellophane behind the door and windows on her cutout. After the glue dries, encourage her to color her schoolhouse, then glue glitter on the bell. When that glue dries, shake off the excess glitter. Mount the schoolhouses on your classroom windows. Your students will soon discover that they can look out their schoolhouse windows and doors and see a world of another color. Hmmm…very interesting!

Ruby Boyatzis—Gr. K
Green Hill International School
Athens, Greece

## Summer Sunflowers

Bring the last rays of summer sunshine into your classroom with these cheery sunflowers. To make a sunflower, paint the bottom of a paper bowl with yellow tempera paint. When the paint has dried, trace the rim of the bowl on yellow construction paper. Cut out the resulting circle. Squeeze a line of glue onto the rim of the bowl; then place the circle on top, covering the open portion of the bowl. Using scraps of yellow construction paper, cut out sunflower petals; then glue them around the circumference of the bowl. Glue sunflower seeds onto the center of the bowl. Attach a green stem and leaf cutouts, and your sunflower will be in full bloom. Brighten your learning environment by displaying the entire crop of sunflowers along a wall. Then watch your youngsters' sunny smiles as they enjoy a tasty treat of sunflower seeds.

Catherine E. Bray—Gr. K, Quadrille Academy, Indio, CA

# A Tree For All Seasons

Branch out with these "tree-mendously" appealing art projects. Use these ideas to create beautiful trees throughout the year. Or, if you are doing a study of all the seasons, have each student create a tree to match his favorite time of the year. To make a tree trunk, cut a 4" x 10" rectangle from the panel of a brown paper bag. Starting at the top center, make a cut halfway down the length of the rectangle. Cut the scrap pieces of the bag into strips of varying lengths and widths. Working at a washable surface, pour a generous amount of glue onto both sides of the rectangle. Spread the glue over the entire piece, working the paper into a trunk with two branches. Press the trunk and branches onto a piece of construction paper. Repeat the gluing, shaping, and pressing process with the scraps to form additional branches. Let the project dry overnight. If desired, color the trunk and branches with brown or black crayons for added color and texture. Choose from the following suggestions to create sensational seasonal trees:

**Fall Foliage:** Press the wet trunk and branches onto dark-green construction paper. Glue small squares of yellow, red, and orange tissue paper onto the branches.

**Winter Wonderland:** Press the trunk and branches onto blue or gray construction paper. Leave the tree bare or dip a small piece of sponge into white paint. Press the sponge onto the branches.

**Spring Blossoms:** Press the trunk and branches onto green construction paper. Pour a small amount of red powder paint into a bag of popcorn; then shake the bag. Glue the popcorn to the tree for blossoms.

**Summer Greenery:** Press the trunk and branches onto yellow construction paper. Tear various shades of green construction paper into small pieces. Glue the scraps onto the branches.

adapted from an idea by Mary E. Maurer, Children's Corner Daycare, Durant, OK

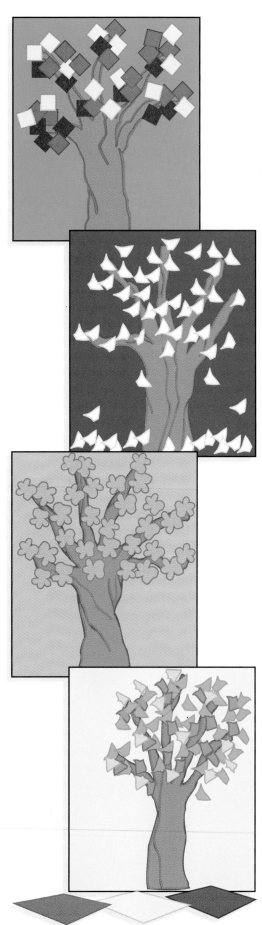

## Fall Foliage

What do asparagus and artichokes have to do with the art process? Plenty—if you're making this fabulous fall foliage. To begin, use an asparagus spear to paint a tree trunk on a sheet of white paper. Then cut approximately one inch off the tops of three different artichokes. Dip one of the artichokes into red, yellow, or orange paint; then press it onto the paper to resemble leaves. Repeat the process as often as you'd like and with the other colors and remaining two artichokes. When the paint is dry, cut around the tree; then mount it on a rich color of construction paper. Have you seen the leaves this year?

Sandie Bolze—Gr. K, Verne W. Critz School
East Patchogue, NY

## Our Class Tree

Each child in your class plays a part in making this spectacular fall display. Begin by peeling the paper off brown crayons. Then give each child one of the peeled crayons and a sheet of paper. Take your students outside and encourage them to look for big trees that have rough bark. Instruct each child to place her paper against the tree bark, then rub the side of the crayon on the paper. Back in the classroom, arrange and tape together all the bark rubbings to resemble a large tree trunk—cutting when necessary. Mount the large tree on a wall. Then encourage each child to paint a piece of paper in any fall color(s). (Sponge-painting also creates a nice effect.) When the paint is dry, have each child trace several leaf patterns onto her paper, then cut them out. Mount all the leaves on the large classroom tree. Spectacular!

Sue Quesenberry, North Hill Elementary School, Rochester, MI

### Fall Foliage Mobile

Your little ones will love the colorful effect of this work of art. To make a leaf mobile, arrange a fresh leaf on a sheet of waxed paper; then add a sprinkling of crayon shavings. Place a second sheet of waxed paper on top of the crayon shavings; then place the sheets between layers of newspaper. Press the sheets together with an iron set on low heat. Remove the waxed paper sheets from the newspaper and let them cool. Next cut loosely around the leaf and punch a hole in the top of the cutout. Personalize each cutout and tie it to a leaf-less tree branch with a length of monofilament line. Suspend this mobile from the ceiling for a colorful fall display.

### It Feels Like Fall

Give youngsters a feel for fall by encouraging them to feel and describe a real tree's trunk and freshly fallen leaves. As a follow-up, have little ones make artistic fall trees. Glue torn, brown construction-paper strips onto a large sheet of finger-painting paper to resemble the rough trunk and branches of a tree. Randomly drop spoonfuls of different colors of liquid tempera paint onto the paper. Cover the paper with a large sheet of waxed paper; then press and rub the paint. Allow the paint to dry completely; then peel away the waxed paper. Cut around the shape of the tree and its brightly colored, leaf-filled branches. Now it feels *and* looks like fall!

Bernadette Hoyer—Pre-K
Coles and McGinn Schools
Scotch Plains, NJ

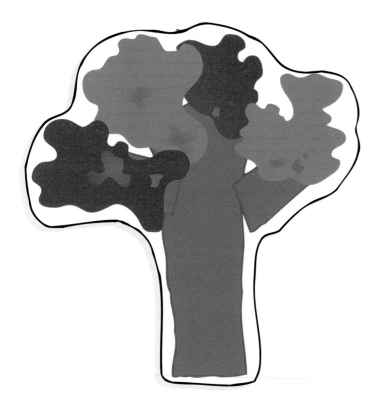

## Autumn Windsocks

Adorn your classroom with these autumn windsocks. In advance collect a supply of brightly colored leaves, or photocopy the leaf patterns on page 100 onto construction paper; then cut them out. To make a windsock, glue the leaves onto a 12" x 18" sheet of construction paper. Allow the glue to dry; then staple the sides of the paper together to form a cylinder. Cut crepe-paper streamers into varying lengths and attach them along the bottom edge of the paper. At the top, punch two holes on each side of the sock; then thread string through the holes and suspend the windsock from the ceiling.

Mary Delak—Gr. K, Washington Elementary School, Ely, MN

## Crafty Theme Tees

Encourage youngsters to show off your class's themes on these terrific T-shirts. Ask each child to bring an oversized, washed, solid-colored T-shirt from home. Have each child personalize his shirt using a fabric pen. To decorate his shirt after each unit or theme, have each child use fabric paint to make a small, theme-related picture on his shirt. Use a fabric pen to label each theme if desired. At the end of the year, this special shirt is bound to be a treasured keepsake.

Dawn Moore—Grs. K–1, Mt. View Elementary
Thorndike, ME

## You've Been Framed

Here's a craft idea you can try when school pictures arrive. To get started on the project, glue a school picture to the center of a rectangle cut from plastic-grid craft canvas (available in a variety of colors at craft stores). Using a child's safety needle, weave brightly colored ribbons and cording through the canvas and around the picture. Attach a length of ribbon for hanging. What a perfect gift for National Grandparents Day!

Betty Silkunas
Oak Lane Day School
Blue Bell, PA

## Fall All Around

You'll rake up piles of creative ways to display these leaves. Collect a supply of large paper grocery bags; then cut out the bottom and down one side of each bag. Thoroughly wet the paper and crumple it. Spread the paper flat to dry. Cut leaf shapes out of the paper; then sponge-paint the leaves a variety of fall colors. When the paint is dry, arrange the leaves as a border around a display. Or mount a supply on a wall to resemble a large wreath. To make an individual wreath, glue a construction-paper wreath shape onto an identically shaped cardboard shape. Glue an arrangement of the leaves atop the wreath. Autumn is all around!

Mary Marcucci—Preschool
Home Childcare
Chandler, AZ

## Colorful Cutouts

Your little ones will love the colorful effect of these fall leaves. To make one, cut out a leaf shape from a coffee filter. Place a few drops of different-colored food coloring (such as orange, yellow, and red) and a few drops of water on a Styrofoam meat tray. Lay the leaf cutout on the meat tray, then set the leaf aside to dry. To vary this activity, fill each of several empty spray bottles with diluted food coloring; then mist a leaf cutout with different colors. Mount the leaves on a wall or bulletin board for a fun fall display.

Donna Henry, Portsmouth, VA

## Fall Leaf Prints

Adorn your classroom with this array of colorful fall foliage. In advance, collect a variety of fall leaves. To make a leaf print, paint the back of a leaf with brown, yellow, orange, red, or green paint. Place the leaf—paint side down—on a large sheet of construction paper. Lay a sheet of newspaper atop the leaf; then gently press and rub it. Remove the newspaper and leaf to reveal the print. Repeat this process several times, using different colors of paint.

Melissa L. Mapes—Pre-Kindergarten
Little People Land Preschool
St. Petersburg, FL

## Scarecrows!

These child-made scarecrows add an adorable seasonal flair to your classroom. To make a scarecrow, stuff a lunch bag with newspaper. Tie off the bag at the top; then paint it. When the paint is dry, fringe-cut the top of the bag to resemble hair, and draw or paint on a face. Then cut out a simple body shape (similar to the one shown) from tagboard or thin cardboard. Place the body on a piece of seasonal fabric or burlap; then loosely trace around the body to make an outline for the scarecrow's outfit. Cut out the outfit; then glue it to the body. Staple the paper-bag head to the long strip at the top of the body. Then mount the finished projects along your classroom wall.

Sheila Neupauer—Gr. K, Ellwood City Children's Center
Ellwood City, PA

## Jack-O'-Lanterns

These jack-o'-lanterns will add a festive touch to Halloween happenings. In advance, purchase a classroom supply of two-inch clay planting pots. To make a jack-o'-lantern, paint the clay pot orange. When the paint dries, turn the pot upside down; then use black Slick® paint to make a jack-o'-lantern face on it. Suspend each of the pots from a length of yarn and hang them from the ceiling. Jack-o'-lanterns everywhere!

Becky Gibson Watson, Camp Hill, AL

## Time To Harvest The Pumpkins

Youngsters are sure to enjoy harvesting this patch of pumpkins. Squirt orange tempera paint into a thoroughly cleaned milk jug. Replace the lid. Shake the jug until it is coated with paint. After removing the top to allow the paint to dry, spray-paint the top green. If desired, add personality to the pumpkin by gluing on paper shapes. Display the patch of pumpkins in an open area among large paper leaves and crepe-paper vines.

Gina Blair—Preschool/Title I
Morning Sun Elementary
Morning Sun, IA

## Fingerpainted Frights

These jack-o'-lanterns are frightfully fun for little fingers to paint. To make one, paint a large piece of paper with a mixture of yellow and orange fingerpaint. When the paint is dry, cut the paper into a pumpkin shape. To make the eyes, the nose, and a grin, press a hand into black paint, then onto the pumpkin as desired. Top the pumpkin with a paper stem. Aren't these the most handsome grins you've seen?

Vickie Zalk—Three-Year-Olds
Hope Creative Preschool, Winter Haven, FL

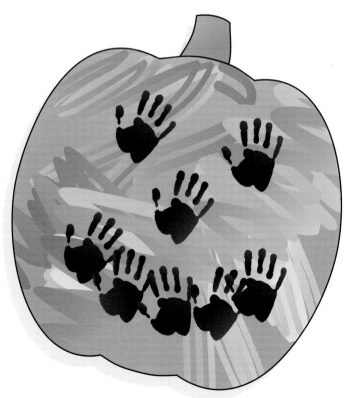

### What Are You Going To Be?

Imaginations, creativity, and problem solving will be in full swing with this art project in which the sky's the limit! First engage a child in a conversation regarding what he would like "to be" for Halloween. To make the character, have the child paint a large shopping bag (with handles) to resemble the character's body. Together brainstorm how the child could create that particular character. Then, choosing from a supply of art materials—such as fabric scraps, tissue paper, ribbon, construction paper, foam balls, etc.—have him create his character's likeness. These projects are definite crowd pleasers!

Barbara Meyers—Gr. K, Fort Worth Country Day
Fort Worth, TX

### Beaming Jack-O'-Lanterns

Illuminate your classroom with these glowing jack-o'-lanterns. To make one, cut or tear orange tissue paper into small pieces. Brush Mod Podge® on a plastic margarine lid; then layer the tissue paper atop the lid. Glue on construction-paper cutouts to make a jack-o'-lantern face. To the top of the lid, glue green tissue paper or curling ribbon; then brush on another layer of Mod Podge®. When dry, peel the tissue paper from the lid. Then punch a hole at the top of the jack-o'-lantern and tie a length of yarn through the hole. Hang these beaming jack-o'-lanterns on your classroom windows. Stunning!

Jane Kjosen, Underwood Elementary
Menomonee Falls, WI

## Pumpkin Tambourine

Celebrate the harvest by shaking a pumpkin tambourine! To make one, paint the backs of two paper plates orange. When the paint is dry, secure the rims of the plates together with several paper clips; then use a hole puncher to punch an even number of holes through the rims. Remove the paper clips. Through every pair of holes, thread a length of green yarn through both plates. Thread a jingle bell onto the yarn; then tie the yarn in a bow. Shake, shake, shake that tambourine!

## Torn Up About Jack-O'-Lanterns

Here's a Halloween idea your youngsters will love to get torn up about. Play some Halloween music or a story tape as you have youngsters tear orange, yellow, and green tissue paper into small pieces. To create this illuminating masterpiece, draw a circle on black construction paper and spread glue to fill the circle. Press enough orange paper pieces on the glue to cover it; then glue the yellow paper atop the orange paper to create a jack-o'-lantern's face. Add a green paper stem in the same manner. How's that for haunting results?

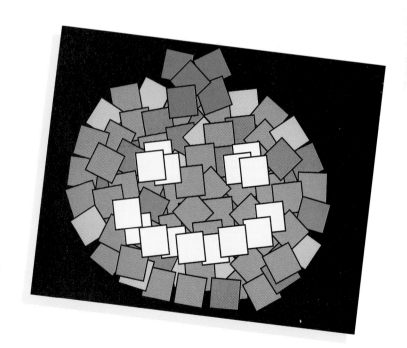

## Spider Wear

Creepy crawlers will be popping up all over when you make these spider hats. Measure and cut a black tagboard strip to fit around each child's head. Staple the ends of the strip together to make a headband. Have each child cut eight strips of black construction paper, then accordion-fold each strip. Staple four of the strips to one side of the headband and four strips to the other. Now your little ones are ready for spider wear!

Cathy Gust—Gr. K
Stiegel Elementary School
Manheim, PA

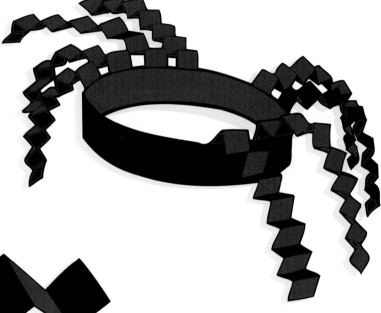

## Halloween Windsocks

These windsocks will add an attractive seasonal flair to any classroom. To make a windsock, dip a Halloween or seasonal cookie cutter into a thin layer of paint, colored glue, or glitter glue; then repeatedly press the design onto a 12" x 18" sheet of orange, white, or black construction paper. Continue in this manner using different cookie cutters. When dry, roll the paper into a loose tubelike shape; then staple it. Punch a hole on each side of the top of the windsock tube. Tie a length of string in each of the holes; then bring the two pieces of string together and knot their ends. Attach tissue-paper streamers to the bottom of the windsock.

Betsy Ruggiano—Three-Year-Olds
Featherbed Lane School
Clark, NJ

## Jack-O'-Lanterns With Panache

These tissue-paper pumpkins will be nifty additions to any classroom. To make one, bend a hanger into a circular shape. Place the hanger atop a sheet of orange tissue paper so that the hook of the hanger extends past the top of the paper. Glue around the inside and outside edges of the hanger. Place another sheet of tissue paper on top of the hanger and press the two sheets together with the hanger in between. When the glue dries, trim the excess paper from around the hanger. Use construction paper to make facial features for the jack-o'-lantern. Mount the finished projects and construction-paper vines on a wall or bulletin board.

## Kitty Bags

Your little trick-or-treaters will be excited to make one of these "kitty" Halloween bags. To make a bag, cut a three-inch strip from the top of a paper grocery bag and set the strip aside for later. Then cut three inches down from each corner of the bag. Fold the tops down to the inside of the bag. Use the three-inch strip to make a handle. Next use black tempera paint to paint the outside of the bag. When the paint dries, use Slick® paint or construction-paper cutouts to make the cat's eyes and nose on the bag. Glue on accordion-folded construction-paper strips to resemble whiskers and construction-paper triangles for ears. "Meeeeeee-ow!"

Carol Bruckner—Gr. K
Oaklawn Elementary
Fort Worth, TX

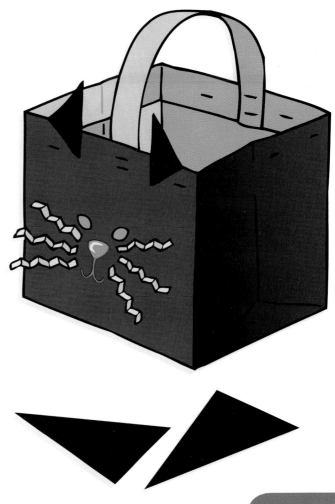

## Plenty Of Pumpkin, Plenty Of Seeds!

That's what youngsters will find when you give them the opportunity to dig into a pumpkin. It's also what they'll find when they peek into this crafty pumpkin! From construction paper, cut a stem, a leaf, and two identically shaped pumpkins. Title one of the pumpkin cutouts "What's Inside A Pumpkin?"; then glue on the stem and leaf. To one side of the other pumpkin cutout, glue short pieces of orange yarn and real pumpkin seeds that have been washed and dried. Assemble the shapes with a brad as shown; then take a pumpkin peek!

Sonja M. Harrington—Pre-K
Tiny Tears Day Care
Albemarle, NC

## Indian Corn

After examining some real Indian corn, have your youngsters decorate your classroom with their own artistic renderings. To make one set of corn, cut out one or more construction-paper ears of corn. (If desired, provide a tagboard tracer or use the pattern on page 101.) Using Q-tips®, paint on red, yellow, orange, and brown kernels. When the paint is dry, arrange and staple the tops of the ears together. Then collect leaves or cornhusks and tape them to the back of the corn (at the top). Make a paper or ribbon bow; then attach it to the front of the corn. Display the finished projects on a tall construction-paper cornstalk.

Karen Badon, Child's Voice School, Elmhurst, IL

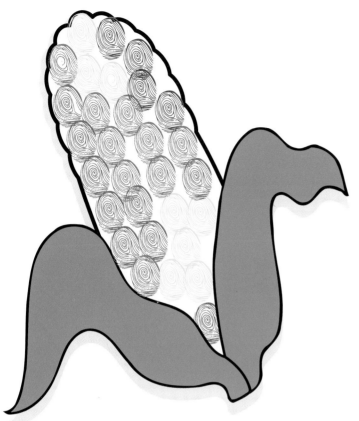

## A Crop Of Corn

Harvest a crop of Indian corn with this fun activity. To make an ear, reproduce the corncob pattern on page 101 onto white construction paper; then cut it out. Dip your finger into red, orange, yellow, brown, or black tempera paint and then onto the cob cutout. Continue in this manner, using different colors until the cutout is covered. When the paint is dry, complete the project by gluing construction-paper cornhusks (or real ones) to each side of the cutout.

## A Real "Corn-ucopia"

With a little shucking and painting, this "cornucopia" is bound to be a big hit. In advance, purchase Indian corn and fresh corn still in the husks. Shuck the corn. If you're using Indian corn, have youngsters shell it and use just the cob for this project. To make a cornucopia, dip either the ear of corn or the corncob into a shallow pan of brown tempera paint. On a sheet of construction paper, press and roll or drag the corn or cob to make a cornucopia-shaped design. Then roll several of the cornhusks into ball shapes and secure the ends with rubber bands. Dip a husk ball in a shallow pan of tempera paint; then repeatedly press it onto the paper near the cornucopia to resemble fruits and vegetables. Continue in this manner several times, using a different color of paint for each cornhusk ball. It's harvesttime!

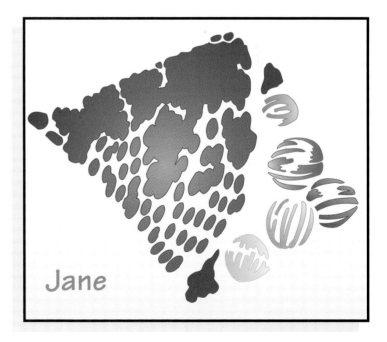

Jane

Donna Selling and Brenda vonSeldeneck—Pre-Kindergarten
First Presbyterian Preschool, Waynesboro, VA

## Turkey On A Platter

This turkey is already on a paper-plate platter and ready to serve as a Thanksgiving delight! Using different colors of tempera paint, sponge-paint a paper plate; then set the plate aside to dry. Using markers or crayons, decorate a pear-shaped, brown cutout to resemble a turkey's body. Glue the cutout to the plate. Better watch out! This turkey's so stunning he'll strut right off the table!

Gail Moody—Preschool
Atascadero Parent Education Preschool
Atascadero, CA

I am thankful for my new baby sister.

John

## Wreath Of Thanks

Parents will be thankful for these decorative harvest wreaths and the sentiments written on them. To make a wreath, glue a construction-paper circle to the center of a paper plate. Glue crumpled squares of tissue paper around the rim of the plate; then glue a bow-shaped cutout to the bottom of the wreath. If desired, attach a small photo of each child to the bow on his wreath. In the center of the wreath, write the child's dictated sentence of thankfulness. To prepare the wreath for hanging, tape a length of ribbon to the back of the plate.

Debi Luke—Three- And Four-Year-Olds
Fairmount Nursery School
Syracuse, NY

All turkey birds are different,
From sea to shining sea.
And you'll never see another bird
Like this one to you from me.
Can you see what makes him different?
Do you need some helpful hints?
I made him from my very own
Thumb and fingerprints!
—*Marsha A. Burks*

## Fingerprint Turkeys

Now these fingerprint turkeys are something to gobble about! In advance, collect different brightly colored, non-toxic stamp pads. To make a turkey, press your thumb or finger onto a stamp pad, then onto a sheet of construction paper. Continue in this manner until the prints resemble the body of a turkey or a circular shape. Press another finger onto a different-colored stamp pad, then repeatedly onto the paper to resemble a row of turkey feathers. Continue in this manner, using a different color for each row of feathers. Then use a fine-tip marker to draw features on the fingerprints so that the picture resembles a turkey. Add to this great gobbler by gluing a copy of the poem (page 102) to the bottom of each paper.

Marsha A. Burks—Grs. K–1, Sheffield Elementary, Lynchburg, VA

## Terrific Turkeys

Your little ones will have lots of fun when you set them loose on these grand gobblers. To make one, trace the turkey head (page 102) onto a folded sheet of construction paper. Also trace the tail on construction paper; then cut on the resulting outlines. Decorate the tail cutout with craft items such as glitter glue, Slick® paint, tissue paper, markers, crayons, feathers, or sequins and set it aside to dry. Glue wiggle eyes and a tissue-paper wattle on the turkey's head. Fold the tabs on the head cutout and glue it to the front of a paper cup. Glue the turkey's tail to the back of the cup. Fill the cup with the candy or nuts of your choice. Display the completed projects in your classroom; then have each child take his turkey home for the Thanksgiving holiday. Gobble, gobble!

Mary E. Maurer, Caddo, OK

## Let's Talk Turkey

If these turkeys could talk, don't you wonder what they'd say? Glue a wooden ice-cream spoon onto the center of a brown paper circle. Then glue colorful construction-paper feathers to the edge of the brown circle. Finish the turkey by gluing wiggle eyes, a paper beak, and a wattle to the spoon. Gobble, gobble! Eat more vegetables, please!

Charlene Vonnahme—Preschool
Carroll Area Child Care Center
Carroll, IA

## I Spy Pumpkin Pie

I spy pumpkin pie—and smell pie, too! These crafty pumpkin pies smell just like the real thing. Fill a paper bowl with torn, orange tissue-paper pieces. Spray the pieces with cinnamon-scented air freshener. While the pieces are damp, sprinkle on pumpkin-pie spice. Trace the top of an empty bowl onto a piece of orange paper; then cut out the circle. Punch holes through the circle; then glue the circle onto the rim of the "pumpkin-filled" bowl. Present these air fresheners as gifts, and spicy thank-yous are sure to follow.

adapted from an idea by Charlet Keller—Preschool
ICC Preschool, Violet Hill, AR

## A Decorative Gobbler Centerpiece

Now these turkeys are worth gobbling about! To make a turkey, use pinking shears to cut a large half-circle from orange construction paper and a slightly smaller half-circle from brown construction paper. Then cut a turkey body, a square for the beak, and turkey feet from construction paper. Use a hole puncher to punch two circles for eyes. Glue the eyes and the turkey feet to the turkey's body. Fold the square to create a triangular-shaped beak; then glue the beak to the body. Attach a length of red curling ribbon to the beak to represent a wattle. Then glue the body to the smaller half-circle and the smaller half-circle to the larger half-circle. Staple a tagboard strip to the back of the turkey pattern. Next wrap the strip around a small pumpkin or vase filled with fresh flowers, sizing it accordingly. Then staple the ends of the tagboard strip. Display the completed projects in your classroom; then have each child take his turkey home for the Thanksgiving holiday. Gobble, gobble!

Ruth Meryweather—Three- and Four-Year-Olds
Uncasville, CT

## Tootsy Turkeys

These tootsy turkeys will wiggle your little ones' toes. In advance mix brown paint with liquid soap in a shallow pan. To make a turkey, step one bare foot into the tray, then onto a 12" x 18" sheet of construction paper. Allow the paint to dry. With the toes facing down, draw or paint feathers around the foot. Then use markers to draw facial features on the footprint to resemble a turkey. Too cute!

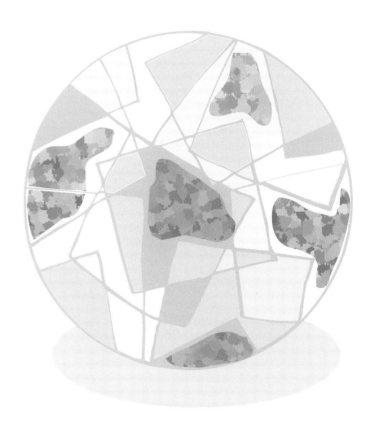

### Snowballs

Displaying these snowballs will create a spectacular winter sight. To make a snowball, place a Styrofoam® ball in the bottom part of an egg carton to prevent the ball from rolling. Brush the upper half of the ball with thinned white glue; then place white and blue tissue-paper squares on the glue. Brush glue on the tissue paper and add additional squares so that they overlap the others. Sprinkle silver or clear glitter sparingly over the wet surface. Allow the glue to dry and repeat the process to complete the other half of the ball. It's a snowball to keep!

### The Invisible Snowman

Young children are fascinated by the results of this fun winter project. From construction paper, cut a hat, eyes, a nose, pieces of coal, and a scarf or shapes for creating a scarf. Arrange the pieces on the adhesive side of a large square of clear Con-Tact® covering to resemble a snowman. Gently press an identically sized piece of Con-Tact® atop the first piece. Cut around the arranged pieces, shaping the area between the hat and the scarf to resemble the snowman's head. Hang the projects with monofilament line from your ceiling or tape them to a window. These snowpeople are sure to be oh, so popular. And the best part is that they never melt!

Kathy Burrows—18-Month-Olds to Six-Year-Olds
Country Meadows Child Care
Bridgeville, PA

## Waiting For Snow?

Wait no more! Create a blizzard of snowflakes in your classroom with this unique printing idea. Cut an orange in half horizontally; then blot the halves dry with a paper towel. Pour light blue tempera paint into trays. To make a snowflake, dip an orange half into the paint. Press the orange onto the center of a sheet of white construction paper to create a unique print. Sprinkle the wet print with clear glitter, if desired. When the paint is dry, cut a simple snow-flake shape around the print. Punch a hole in the shape; then tie on a length of yarn. Hang the flurry of flakes from your ceiling. It's snowing!

Anne Oeth—Preschool, Rockwell Preschool, Omaha, NE

## Winter Stars

Your classroom will twinkle with these stars that are reminiscent of a crisp, clear winter sky. To make a star, paint eight craft sticks the color of your choice. Sprinkle the wet paint with glitter. When the paint is dry, shake off the excess glitter. Then use hot glue to glue the craft sticks together—similar to an asterisk. When the glue is dry, hot-glue a ribbon to one of the sticks for hanging. Twinkle! Twinkle!

Linda Schwitzke—Headstart
Longview, WA

## Frosty Friends

Recycling comes into play in making these frosty friends. In advance, collect an empty, clean plastic jar (such as the 20 oz. powdered-drink-mix containers) and an old sport sock for each child. Provide craft glue, permanent markers, and various art supplies such as sequins, pom-poms, and buttons. To make one frosty friend, stretch the sock over the top of the jar to resemble a hat (if necessary, cut the toe off the sock). Then glue on craft items and draw features to create a unique frosty friend. Display these cute fellows in a winter wonderland scene complete with white packing-foam snow.

Debbie Amason—Gr. K
West End Elementary School
Milledgeville, GA

## Marvelous Matching Mittens

Match this art project with a winter unit and you'll have an activity that is sure to be a winner! Trace a mitten pattern onto a folded sheet of construction paper. Cut out the mitten shape through both thicknesses. Using eyedroppers, drop several different colors of liquid tempera paint onto one of the mitten cutouts. Place the matching mitten atop the painted mitten and press. Pull the mittens apart and set them aside to dry. Laminate, then place each child's mittens in a center for use as a matching activity. Or attach string to each child's mittens. Tie each pair of mittens to a longer length of string to drape across a door or bulletin board.

Cheryl Cicioni—Preschool
Kindernook Preschool
Lancaster, PA

## Dressed For The Weather

Youngsters can head out into the snow with style when wearing these snazzy shirts. To design one, prewash a black or dark blue sweatshirt. Using white fabric paint, paint the bottom of a child's foot; then have him press his footprint onto the front of the shirt. Using squeezable white fabric paint that dries shiny, outline the footprint and create a border of snow as shown. When this paint is dry, invite the child to complete the shirt by using various colors of squeezable paint to add features to the snowman and snowflakes to the background. This snowman is really stylin'!

Jody Johnson—Preschool
Little Lamb Preschool
Madison, SD

## Cool Dude

This winter guy requires some assistance to make, but the result is really cool! Cut a strip of quilt batting to match the circumference and height of a plastic container such as those used to package powdered drink mix. Brush the sides of the container with craft glue; then press the strip onto the container. Glue wiggle eyes, a yarn mouth, and a felt carrot nose to the batting. Tie a strip of fabric or length of ribbon around the snowman. To make a top hat for the snowman, tape the ends of a strip of construction paper together to create a tube; then tape the tube onto a paper circle. Or top this snow dude off with a miniature straw hat (available at craft stores).

Susan Hammett and Marilyn Blair—Pre-K
Cedar Springs Preschool
Knoxville, TN

## "Scent-sational" Gingerbread Folk

Youngsters will run, run, as fast as they can to do this fun gingerbread-person art activity. To make one, copy the gingerbread person pattern (page 103) onto tagboard and cut it out. Then trace it onto the back of an 8" x 10" sheet of sandpaper. Using sharp, blunt-nosed scissors, cut out the sandpaper pattern. Rub a cinnamon stick across the rough side of the cutout. Then, using a mixture of white glue and white paint, decorate the gingerbread person. Attach a bow for the finishing touch. Mount these decorative gingerbread folk on a bulletin board to fill your room with the fragrance of cinnamon.

Sandie Bolze—Gr. K
Verne W. Critz School
East Patchogue, NY

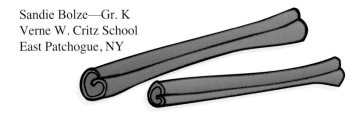

## Stir Up A Treat

That's what parents will be able to do when they receive these tasty stirring spoons. To begin melt colored confectionery coating according to package directions. Invite each child to thoroughly cover the bowl of a plastic spoon by dipping it into the melted coating. Place the spoon bowl-side-up on a piece of waxed paper to cool. After the coating is firmly set on the spoon (about two hours), help the student secure a piece of colored plastic wrap around the coated end of the spoon with a holiday ribbon. Tape a packet of hot cocoa mix to the spoon; then send the stirring delight home with each child to give to his parent. Yummy!

Sue Lewis Lein—Four-Year-Olds
St. Pius X
Wauwatosa, WI

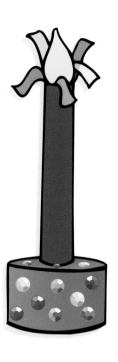
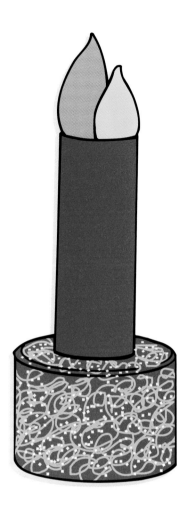

## Holiday Candles

Candlelight is glowing bright on these joyous holiday nights. To make a candle, roll a piece of construction paper into a tube; then tape it together. Cut flames from construction paper or tissue paper; then glue them inside the top of the candle. Decorate a spray-can top by spray-painting it, attaching stickers, or using glitter glue. Using a thick stream of glue, center the candle on top of the decorated top. When the glue is dry, display these holiday candles around your classroom.

Dianne Joseph—Gr. K
Bayou Vista Elementary
Morgan City, LA

## Handy Menorah

Students' eyes will light up with excitement when they make these handsome menorahs. To make one, trace both hands onto a piece of yellow construction paper. Cut out the hand shapes; then glue them on a piece of blue construction paper so that the shapes of the pinkies overlap. Cut white paper flames; then glue a flame atop each of the candles. If desired, add glitter to the flames so they shine brightly throughout the season. Happy Hanukkah!

Lori J. Kracoff—Preschool
The Curious George Cottage Learning Center
Waterville Valley, NH

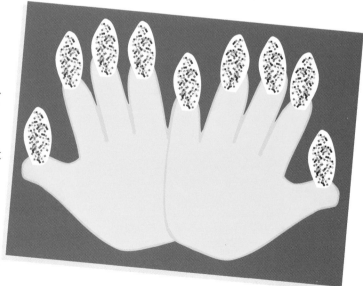

## Cup Coaster

Each of your youngsters will be proud to present this pretty cup coaster to her parent. To create a coaster, cut out a design or a panel from a holiday napkin. Then paint the top of a ceramic tile square with glue. Position the napkin cutout on the glue. Sprinkle iridescent glitter around the cutout. After the glue dries, spray the tile with several coats of an acrylic sealer (available at craft stores). After the sealer dries thoroughly, attach felt-pad feet to the bottom of the coaster with craft glue. There you have it—a cool coaster for a hot drink!

Mary Siano—Special Education Grs. 1–3
William Floyd Elementary School
Shirley, NY

## Antique Photos

Here's a great project that little ones can give as holiday gifts. In advance use black-and-white film to photograph each child wearing clothing such as floppy hats, boas, jewelry, oversized coats, vests, dresses, and sweaters. Have the film developed. Glue each photo to a piece of black poster board. Have each of your students glue items such as lace, ribbon, pearls, sequins, buttons, old jewelry, and doilies to the poster board. There you have it! An antique-looking memento that is sure to be a treasure.

Carol Hargett—Four-Year-Olds, Kinderhaus III, Fairborn, OH

## Child-Made Gift Bags

Youngsters will beam with pride at their handiwork on these gift bags. For each child, cut a rectangular piece of burlap large enough to fold in half. In advance, dip the burlap edges in water-diluted glue (to prevent unraveling); then let the glue dry. Thread a blunt tapestry needle with yarn. Demonstrate a basic running stitch by showing youngsters how to move the needle through the fabric in an alternating up-and-down pattern. Then have each child sew around three edges of his folded fabric, leaving the top edge open. Help each child tie off the end of his yarn. To close each bag, use a large safety pin that has a colorful ribbon tied to it.

Wilma Droegemueller—Gr. K and Preschool
Zion Lutheran School
Mt. Pulaski, IL

## Fridge Fancies

Parents will love the personal flair their children give to these refrigerator memo pads. To make a pad backing, punch holes around the edges of a 5" x 8" piece of cardboard. Sponge-paint or stamp ink designs on the backing. Secure the end of a length of multicolored yarn through one of the holes of the decorated backing; then tie the other end of the yarn to a bobby pin. Lace the yarn through all the holes in the backing, adding yarn lengths as necessary, until all the edges have been laced. Remove the bobby pin; then secure the loose yarn end to the backing. Glue a 3" x 5" notepad to the decorated side of the backing to create a memo pad; then attach a strip of magnetic tape to the back of the pad. Send each child's gift pad home along with his personalized holiday greeting—in memo form!

Betsy Pottey—Gr. K
Early Childhood Center
Abington, MA

For Dad

I love you.

Happy Holidays
From, David

## A Sweet Gift

Have little ones make these sweet treats for holiday gift giving. For each child, supply a clean, plastic container from a beverage mix or frosting. Spray paint the lids with nontoxic paint, if desired. Have each child select from recent artwork, a small drawing, a section of a painting, or a finger-painting sample. Trim it to fit the side of the container. Assist each student in painting Mod Podge® on the exterior of the container, excluding the rim and bottom. Help each child place the artwork on the Mod Podge®. Brush over the artwork with a coat of Mod Podge®. Then have each student sprinkle the entire container with clear or frosted glitter. When the containers are dry, have each of your little ones fill his container with assorted wrapped candy for gift giving.

## "Eggs-tra" Special Wreath

If your holiday cleaning efforts turn up an over-abundant supply of cardboard egg cartons, here's a creative use for them. Cut off and discard the top of each carton; then cut apart the two rows of egg cups lengthwise. To create a wreath, staple the ends of the egg-cup strips together, with the open sides of the cups facing outward. Paint the wreath with green tempera paint. After the paint dries, poke a separate eight-inch square of holiday tissue paper or red plastic wrap into each glue-lined cup. If desired glue a bow and holiday confetti to the wreath. Then hot-glue a ribbon hanger to the back of the wreath. Invite youngsters to display their wreaths at home for that "eggs-tra" holiday touch.

Sheila Crawford—Five-Year-Olds
Kids Kampus
Huntington, IN

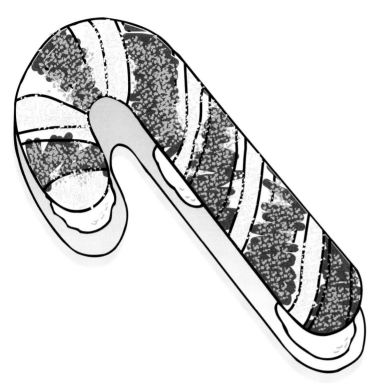

## Scented Candy Canes

These candy canes look good enough to eat—but don't! They are for dazzling decoration purposes only. To make one, cut two identically sized candy-cane shapes from tagboard. Use a permanent black marker to draw section lines on opposites sides of each candy cane. Brush every other section with water-diluted glue; then shake on kosher salt—quite a bit of it. When the glue dries, shake off the excess salt. Then use red tempera paint to paint every other section of the candy canes red. While the paint is still wet, shake on more kosher salt. When the paint dries, shake off the excess salt. Then dip three cotton balls in peppermint extract. Sandwich the cotton balls between the two cutouts; then glue them in place. Use the finished projects to decorate a class-room doorway or wall and scent your room with the pleasing aroma of peppermint.

Rose Semmel
Raritan Valley Community College Child Care
Somerville, NJ

## What An Angel!

Parents are sure to treasure these handmade angels. Begin by painting white handprints onto blue construction paper; then set the prints aside to dry. Cut a circle from the appropriate color of skin-toned construction paper. Glue the circle to a white con-struction-paper triangle. Use markers to draw a face on the circle; then glue on pieces of yarn or tinsel to represent hair. Embellish the angel's robe with materials such as lace, glitter, pearls, sequins, or ribbon flowers. Cut around the shapes of the dry handprints; then glue them to the back of the angel to represent wings. As a finishing touch, twist a pipe cleaner to resemble a halo; then tape it to the back of the angel's head. Heavenly!

Deborah Olsen—Four-Year-Olds
The School Of Grace
Raleigh, NC

## Sleep In Heavenly Peace

When sleeping on these pillows, your little ones will have the sweetest of dreams. Provide a prewashed, white pillowcase for each student, or ask each child to bring one. Before painting a pillowcase, insert a personalized sheet of paper that is the length and width of the pillowcase. Using fabric paint, generously paint a child's hand yellow or gold. Have him press his hand onto the pillowcase to form an angel's wings. After the child's hand has been washed and dried, paint it once more with a different color of his choice. Have him press his hand on the pillowcase again to form the angel's body. Using the appropriate colors, paint a head, hair, a halo, eyes, and a mouth. Add a message, the child's name, and the date. Add additional designs to the pillowcase if desired. Follow the manufacturer's instructions to permanently set the paints if necessary.

Janice Hughes and Jean Bower—Four- And Five-Year-Olds
Messiah Lutheran Nursery School
Williamsport, PA

## We Love Christmas!

Fill your room with candy canes this Christmas. To make one of these sweet hearts, use red paint, crayons, or tissue-paper squares to decorate two construction-paper candy-cane shapes. When the canes are complete, glue the tips together to create a heart. Now that's a candy-cane Christmas!

Beth Lemke—Pre-K
Heights Head Start
Coon Rapids, MN

## Cut It Out!

Your little ones will be crazy about these cut-up Christmas trees! Visually divide the bottom of a green or holiday-designed paper plate into four different-sized triangles. Cut along the lines; then sequence the triangles by size from largest to smallest. Glue the largest triangle—right side up—to a piece of construction paper. Above the triangle, glue the remaining pieces to the paper to form a tree. Top the tree with a paper star shape. If desired, trim the tree with glitter, sequins, or holiday-shaped confetti pieces. Each triangular tree will be in tip-top shape!

Faith Heaviside—Nursery School
Fairmount Nursery School
Syracuse, NY

## "Hand-y" Holiday Prints

Whether it's reindeer or jolly old you-know-who—this idea will come in "hand-y." To make a Santa, assist each youngster in painting the palm of his hand with a selected skin tone of washable paint, and his fingers and thumb with white paint. Then have him press his hand onto a sheet of construction paper. When the paint dries, have him use Slick® fabric paint to add eyes, a nose, a mouth, a mustache, and a hat.

To make a reindeer, assist each child in painting his hand—but not his thumb—brown. Then have him press his hand onto a sheet of construction paper. Direct him to use his finger to spread the paint to "draw" antlers. When the paint dries, have him use Slick fabric paint to make eyes and a nose on the reindeer's face. Mount these cheerful holiday works of art individually or attach them to a large sheet of bulletin-board paper to resemble a quilt.

Judy H. Dixon
Forest School
Owensboro, KY

## Seasonal Wreaths

Grace your hallways, windows, or classroom doors with these child-made wreaths. To make one, paint the edge of a paper plate green. When the paint is dry, fold the plate in half; then cut out the inside. Unfold the plate; then decorate it with red stickers, paint, or glitter glue. Hot-glue a fabric bow to the top. Then punch a hole near the top of the wreath and add a length of yarn for hanging. Deck the halls!

Nina Tabanian—Gr. K
St. Rita School
Dallas, TX

## Dreidel Delight

These dreidels are so unusual, making them will leave your youngsters spinning with delight. Prepare a dreidel template similar to the shape shown. Use a white candle to trace the shape onto white construction paper. Then paint over the shape with watered-down blue tempera paint. While the paint is wet, sprinkle on gold or blue glitter. When the paint is dry, shake off the excess glitter.

Linda Blassingame
JUST 4 & 5 Developmental Laboratory
Mobile, AL

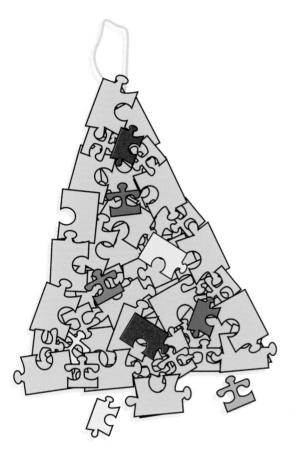

## Puzzle Ornaments

Puzzled over what to do with those boxes of puzzles that are missing a few pieces? Try making these ornaments created from puzzle pieces. To begin, cut out a cardboard holiday shape—such as a bell or tree. Glue several layers of puzzle pieces onto the cutout to cover it completely. Then spray the cutout with gold paint. After the paint dries, glue several more puzzle pieces onto the top layer of the cutout to give the resulting ornament a colorful look. Hot-glue a gold cord hanger to the back of the cutout; then have youngsters decorate the class tree with their ornaments. Before school dismisses for its holiday break, invite each child to wrap her ornament to give as a gift. The puzzle is solved!

Jeanne Jackson—Gr. K
Northside Primary
Palestine, TX

## "Hand-y" Christmas Trees

Deck the halls with these terrific Christmas trees. To make a tree, press a hand into green tempera paint. Keeping the fingers and thumb close together, press the hand onto a sheet of white construction paper to represent tree leaves and branches. Cut a tree trunk from brown paper and glue it under the tree leaves. Then glue a gold or silver foil star to the top of the tree. To complete the project, use glitter glue, paint, or small candies to decorate the tree.

Tammy Bruhn—Pre-K, Ann Arbor, MI

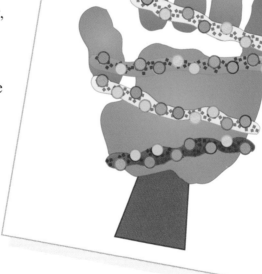

## Hung With Care...Everywhere!

Have your little ones make these eye-catching holiday stockings. To make a stocking ornament, fold a sheet of wallpaper in half. Trace a stocking pattern (or draw one) onto the wallpaper. Cut on the resulting outline through both paper thicknesses; then glue the two cutouts together. Embellish the stocking with pieces of ribbon, lace, sequins, and dried flowers. When the glue has dried, punch a hole near the top of the stocking; then suspend it from a tree using gold cord.

Linda Schwitzke
Headstart Preschool
Longview, WA

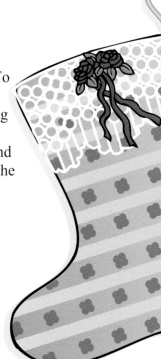

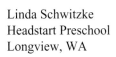

## Darling Dove Decorations

These precious ornaments make darling tree, window, or over-the-door decorations. To begin create tagboard templates from the dove beak, wing, and tail patterns (page 104). For each child trace the wing template twice, and the beak and tail templates once onto a piece of sturdy white cardboard. Cut out each shape; then have the child color the cutouts with a gold crayon. (Or cut the patterns from gold mat board.) Slice off a small piece of a 1 1/2" Styrofoam® ball to create a flat edge. Then, using a toothpick and glue, join the flat edge of the ball to the wide end of a 2 3/8" x 1 7/8" Styrofoam® egg to make a dove. Invite the child to paint her dove with white tempera paint. After the paint dries, have her insert the beak, tail, and wing cutouts into her dove as shown. Hot-glue wiggle eyes onto the dove's head. Create a hanger by gluing both ends of a gold cord into a small hole poked into the dove's back. Then encourage youngsters to delight their parents with these gift-wrapped dove surprises.

Lucia Kemp Henry
Fallon, NV

## Wonderful Wreaths

Your little ones will enjoy making these festive holiday wreaths. To make a wreath, cut the center portion from a nine-inch paper plate. Glue holiday baking cups (turned inside out so that the design is showing) on the plate. When the glue is dry, glue a paper or ribbon bow to the wreath to complete the project. There you have it! A wonderful holiday wreath!

Martha Ann Davis—Gr. K
Springfield Elementary School
Greenwood, SC

## A Tree With A Twist

Here's a tree with a twist. To trim a tagboard tree shape, twist pieces of green tissue paper. Glue the twisted paper to the tree; then top it with glitter-glue garland, paper ornaments, or shiny sequins. What a fantastic, fine-motor fir!

Betsy Ruggiano, Featherbed Lane School, Clark, NJ

## Showy Snowflake Ornaments

The snow must go on! So gather up some fake, dry snow from a craft store and get ready to make these showy ornaments. Glue three miniature pretzels together to resemble the shape of a snowflake. When the glue has dried completely, place the pretzel ornament on a piece of waxed paper and paint both sides white. Once again, let the ornament dry completely. Later dip the painted ornament into glue, then into a shallow container of decorative snow. To complete the ornament, tie a satin ribbon around it for hanging.

Pam H. Tribble—Four-Year-Olds
First Baptist Church
Calhoun, GA

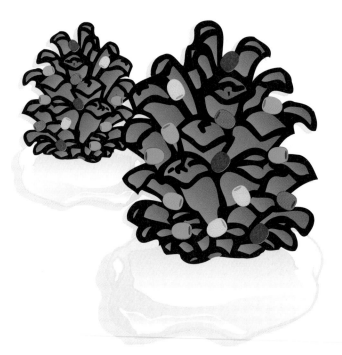

## A Forest Of Decorated Firs

When these projects are displayed together, you'll have a fantastic forest of firs. To make a miniature fir tree, paint a pinecone with green tempera paint. Set the cone aside to dry. Following the package directions, mix a thick batch of plaster of Paris. Drop a large spoonful of the mixture onto a piece of aluminum foil; then press the bottom of the pinecone into the plaster. When the plaster has set, embellish the fir tree by gluing on colorful beads.

Deborah Pruett, Woods Preschool, St. Mary Of The Woods College
St. Mary Of The Woods, IN

### Darling Cherub

Have each of your little angels make a look-alike cherub to give to her mom or dad. Cut an oval from the appropriate color of skin-toned construction paper. Glue the oval atop a gold or silver doily. Use markers to add facial features. Glue a handful of decorative moss to the top of the angel's head. Attach a metallic pipe-cleaner halo to the angel with a paper clip. Heavenly!

Sandra W. Scott—Pre-K
Asheville High Child Care
Asheville, NC

### Corny Kwanzaa Craft

Here's a craft to help add meaning to your celebration of Kwanzaa. Break or cut an ear of corn into thirds. Prepare trays of red, black, and green tempera paint. Use the corn and paint to make creative prints on white construction paper. If desired, write a large *K* on a piece of paper. Print inside the outline of the letter with the corn. *K* is for Kwanzaa!

Dayle Timmons—Special Education Pre-K
Alimacani Elementary School
Jacksonville, FL

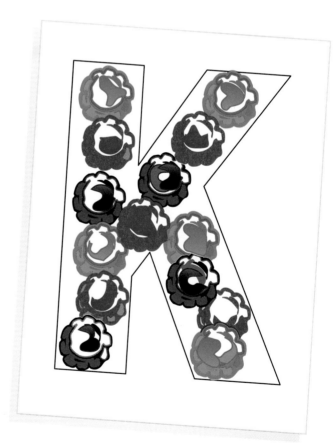

## Soft-Light Candleholders

Youngsters can contribute to the mood of their holiday celebrations when they share these sweet candleholders with their families. To begin have each child glue tissue-paper pieces onto a small baby-food jar. After the glue dries, instruct her to paint a coat of glue over the jar. Set the jar aside until the glue is completely dry; then put a votive candle or tea light into the candleholder. Invite the child to wrap her candleholder in several layers of holiday tissue paper, then place it in a paper bag. Help her tie a holiday ribbon around the top of the bag; then attach a note suggesting that this special gift be opened and used during a holiday celebration. It's a soft touch for some busy times.

Heather Scott—Pre-K
Puddle Duck Daycare
Woburn, MA

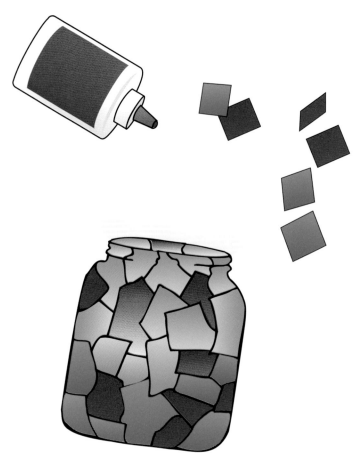

## Living In Harmony

In honor of Martin Luther King, Jr.'s birthday, create these colorful crafts that convey his message of peace and unity. In advance photocopy the people patterns on page 104. Then use that copy to reproduce the patterns on various colors of construction paper. To make one project, use a permanent marker to roughly draw land shapes on a paper plate. Color the land shapes with a green crayon, pressing down hard. Then paint over the whole plate with water-diluted blue tempera paint. When the paint is dry, cut out various colors of the people patterns and glue them to the plate. Display the finished projects on a bulletin board titled "Living In Harmony."

Peg Meehan, Mrs. M's Playcare, Narragansett, RI

### Hello, Mr. Groundhog

It's time for that furry little guy to come peeking out of his hole! This February, have youngsters make these groundhog projects to do a little peeking of their own. To make one, cut the center out of a small paper plate, leaving just the rim. Color or paint the rim green or brown. Then fold down the top of a paper lunch bag and staple the plate rim to the folded-down section of the bag. Use the patterns on page 105 to make construction-paper groundhogs or have children create original groundhogs from art materials. Snuggle the groundhog in his burrow (bag). On February 2, will the groundhog see his shadow? Take a peek and see!

Rose Semmel, Stanton Learning Center, Stanton, NJ

### Got Valentines?

Get ready for your valentine exchange with these handled heart holders. To make a holder, remove the label from a clean, empty milk jug. Use a permanent red marker to draw a large heart on the front of the jug. Use scissors to cut down the jug's sides and around the top of the heart, leaving the handle intact as shown. Personalize the back panel of the jug. Decorate the holder by gluing red, pink, and white tissue-paper pieces on the heart shape. If desired, punch holes around the cut edges and lace the holder with colored yarn.

Linda Kirk—Preschool
Rainbow Child Care Center, Bakersfield, CA

### Valentine Pockets

Looking for a creative way for youngsters to make their own valentine holders? Pick this pocket idea! Using pinking shears, cut off a third of a paper plate. Staple the larger cut plate to a full plate to make a pocket. Beginning at the top of the pocket, use a hole puncher to punch an even number of holes along the rims of the plates. Lace the plates together with a yard of red yarn. When you've finished lacing, tie the yarn into a loop at the top of the pocket. Decorate the pocket using paper heart cutouts and heart-shaped doilies. As a final touch, personalize the pocket and glue on a photo.

Elaine Dittman—Preschool
Holy Trinity Lutheran Preschool
Chicora, PA

### Still Snowing?

If you love winter, you'll be delighted with these lovely valentine snowflake wreaths. Prepare several snowflake templates to be used as stencils. (Or purchase decorative snowflakes from a party-supply store.) To make a wreath, cut a large hexagon from white tagboard. Place a template on the tagboard; then sponge-paint the hexagon using pastel-colored paints. Arrange and press paper heart cutouts onto the wet paint. When the paint is dry, punch a hole through the top of the wreath; then tie on a length of yarn to make a loop. Invite parents to hang the wreaths on their doors as a "heart-y" winter welcome.

Brenda vonSeldeneck and Donna Selling—Four-Year-Olds
First Presbyterian Preschool
Waynesboro, VA

## A Valentine's Day Card

This Valentine's Day card sure is a keeper! To make one, have each child draw a head-and-neck outline on skin-toned construction paper. Supply each child with a 2 1/2" x 18" strip of tagboard. Have each youngster trace both of his hands, then cut on the resulting outlines. Have him glue a hand cutout to each end of the tagboard strip, then glue the strip to the bottom of the head-and-neck cutout to re-semble arms. Encourage each child to color and decorate the head pattern to resemble himself and color the arms as desired. Fold the arms towards the middle, overlapping them. Program each part of the card as shown.

Sharon Kudirko—Grs. K–2
Cooper School
Sheboygan, WI

## A Card With Heart

This sweet valentine card is sure to warm anybody's heart. To make a card, copy the poem shown onto white paper; then photocopy a classroom supply. To make a card, have each child glue a copy of the poem on a folded sheet of pink construction paper, then use crayons to make a decorative border. On a red sheet of construction paper, have each child trace both hands; then have him complete the drawing by rounding the bottom of both palms. Instruct each child to cut on the resulting outlines. Direct him to glue his school photo on the inside of the card. Then have him glue on just the palms of his hand cutouts (overlapping them as shown) to resemble a heart over his photo. What a heartwarming surprise!

Marsha A. Burks—Pre-K, Gr. K, and Special Education
Sheffield School
Lynchburg, VA

Most holidays our teacher
Has us do some special art.
You can see our hands and fingerprints,
But do you see our hearts?

You cannot see a "heart-print,"
But our hearts are there each time.
So please accept my little heart,
In this special valentine.

Love,
Ben

Love,
Ben

### Heart-To-Heart Bookmarks

Youngsters will put their hearts into making these special bookmarks to keep or give away. To make one you will need two 7" x 2 1/2" construction-paper strips—one white and one the color of your choice. Brush a coat of diluted white glue onto the white strip. Cover one side of the strip with tissue-paper scraps; then brush on another coat of glue. Next fold the second strip in half lengthwise. Draw half-hearts on the fold as shown. Cut out the hearts; then open the strip. Place that strip on top of the tissue-papered strip, applying more glue if needed. When the glue has dried, laminate the bookmark. Then punch a hole in the top of the bookmark and tie on a length of pretty ribbon. Heart-to-heart bookmarks, ready to go!

Read to your heart's content!

### A Valentine Gift

These valentine keepsakes will surely help youngsters win the hearts of those they love. In advance copy the poem onto white paper; then photocopy a classroom supply onto construction paper. Assist each child in cutting an 8" x 11" piece of lace (or sheer netting). Have each child lay the lace (right side down) on a flat surface and place a handful of potpourri in the center of the lace. Help each child wrap the lace around the potpourri and gather the excess lace. Secure it with a rubber band. As a finishing touch, have each youngster cut a length of ribbon to tie around the sachet. Attach the poem to the sachet.

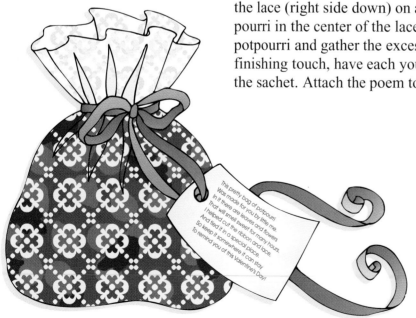

This pretty bag of potpourri
Was made for you by little me.
In it there are leaves and flowers
That will smell sweet for many hours.
I helped cut the ribbon and lace,
And tied it in a special place.
So keep it somewhere it can stay
To remind you of this Valentine's Day!

Tina Summers, North Little Rock, AR

## "Thumb-ody" Loves You!

Loved ones will be touched by the message on these valentine gifts. To make a thumbprint hearts arrangement, cut various sizes of heart shapes from white or pink construction paper. Using red tempera paint, decorate the heart shapes with thumbprints. Set the hearts aside to dry. Personalize and write "Thumb-ody Loves You!" on a 4 1/2" x 8 1/2" piece of white paper. Tape the paper around a clean 12-ounce juice can. Glue a painted heart to the can; then glue the remaining hearts to craft sticks. Press a small amount of clay into the bottom of the deco-rated can; then tuck a section of red tissue paper into the can. Insert the sticks through the paper and into the clay. Isn't it nice to be reminded that "thumb-ody" loves you?

Martha Berry—Two-Year-Olds
Main Street Methodist Preschool
Kernersville, NC

## Lovely Log Cabins

If your class is studying Abraham Lincoln, young-sters will enjoy designing and building these log cabins to mark the occasion. To make one, you will need a sheet of white construction paper, a large supply of pretzel sticks, glue, and crayons. Arrange and glue the pretzel sticks on the paper to resemble a cabin. (If necessary, break the pretzels to achieve the desired effect.) When the glue dries, color a scene around the cabin. (This is a good time to discuss what Abraham Lincoln might have had in his yard. Any swing sets or skateboards in these scenes?) When each project is finished, display them in your classroom. Invite children to discuss how and why they made their cabins the way they did.

Trisha Owen—Grs. K–1
Libbey Elementary School
Wheatland, WY

### ROAR!

Make these "fur-ocious" fine-motor lions just in time for March. On the back of a yellow paper plate, draw lines from the edge of the rim to the edge of the circle as shown. On the front of the plate, use permanent markers to draw a lion's face. Cut along the lines on the rim; then fold forward some of the sections to create the lion's mane. When these lions are displayed together, your students are sure to take pride in their work!

Gail Moody—Preschool
Atascadero Parent Education Preschool
Atascadero, CA

The birdies sing because it's spring,
And bunnies hop, hop, hop.
From below the grass, the flowers wake,
And up their little heads pop.

They greet the trees and warm spring breeze
With a cheery spring hello
To tell the world that spring has sprung
And the winter snow should go.

How wonderful the springtime
With all its life anew.
I hope that this and every spring
Bring happiness to you!

### Spring Has Sprung!

Welcome springtime with a spring picture that's really hands-on! In advance, copy the poem shown onto white paper; then duplicate a class supply on construction paper. To make this springtime scene, add art around the poem by pressing a fingertip on a stamp pad, then onto the construction paper. Continue in this manner—making designs to resemble birds, butterflies, insects, rabbits, flowers, and a sun. Then use a fine-tip marker to add details to your scene. Glue a fringed construction-paper strip at the bottom to resemble grass.

Marsha Burks—Grs. K–2
Sheffield Elementary
Lynchburg, VA

## Creative Kite-Making

During the blustery days of March, decorate your classroom with these kid-made kites. To make them, you will need construction paper, permanent black markers, crepe paper, tempera paints, a few margarine tubs, a few Lincoln Logs®, scissors, and glue. To begin, cut out a construction-paper kite shape. Use the margarine tub and the ends of the Lincoln Logs® to make prints to decorate the kite as desired. When the paint dries, add details with a black marker. Use the length of your arm to measure crepe-paper streamers. Cut the streamers; then glue them on the kite to create the tail. Mount the finished projects along a long length of blue bulletin-board paper. What a beautiful sight in your classroom sky!

Sandy O'Connell—Gr. K
M. M. Pierce
Remington, VA

## Spring Bouquets

Your little ones will learn new art techniques with this creative project. To begin, tear a page from a book of wallpaper samples; then fold it in half either vertically or horizontally. Cutting away from the fold, cut out half of a vase shape freehand. Open the paper and glue the vase cutout to a larger sheet of fingerpaint paper. Using a green marker, draw stems above the vase. Drop spoonfuls of different colors of paint onto the paper on and above the stems. Lay a piece of waxed paper atop the paint; then press, pat, and roll the colors together. When the paint dries, remove the waxed paper. Trim the paper around the vase and bouquet of flowers. Now that's creativity in bloom!

Bernadette Hoyer—Title I Pre-K
Brunner School
Scotch Plains, NJ

## St. Pat's Weave

Over, under, over, under—a little patterning and some artwork make a fine St. Patrick's Day project. To begin, draw or use art supplies to decorate the center of a sturdy paper plate with a St. Pat's theme. Then cut slits around the rim of the plate at approximately two-inch intervals. Knot a length of yarn; then begin weaving it over and under the slits. To attach a new length or color of yarn, just tie it onto the other piece at the back of the plate. When your weaving is complete, secure the end of the yarn by tucking it in the other yarn pieces. Mount the finished projects on a St. Pat's board.

## Leprechaun Mask

Here's just the right costume to promote the St. Patrick's Day mood. For each child, enlarge and photocopy the hat and beard patterns (page 106) on construction paper. (You will need to enlarge the patterns to approximately 115%.) Also provide a variety of art supplies—especially green ones! To make the mask, first use art supplies to decorate the hat as you like. Then fringe-cut the beard. Next glue the beard to the bottom of the hat. Then tape a length of yarn to each side of the hat. Invite your little ones to don their leprechaun masks during your St. Patrick's Day celebrations.

Jeannie Ryan—Gr. K
Provident Heights
Waco, TX

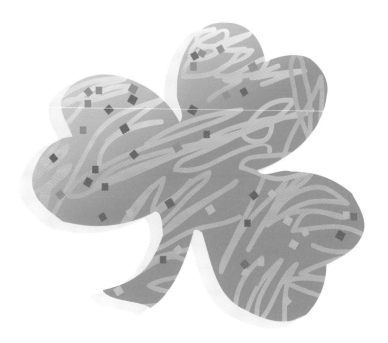

## Shimmering Shamrocks

These shimmering shamrocks are sure to dazzle everyone who catches a glimpse of them. Have each child place a dab of blue and a dab of yellow finger paint atop a sheet of finger-paint paper. Then have him use his fingers to blend the colors together and paint the paper. While the paint is still wet, have each child sprinkle green glitter (and foil pieces if desired) atop the paint. When the paint dries, cut out a shamrock shape from each paper. These sparklers will add a festive touch to any classroom!

Tammy Bruhn—Pre-K
Temperance, MI

## Shamrocks Galore And More!

Excite your little leprechauns with this open-ended art activity. Brush green and white paint onto a large sheet of black construction paper. Press a few shamrock cutouts into the wet paint. If desired, also add glitter and metallic confetti. When the paint is dry, mount the artwork on a larger sheet of green paper. Adapt this idea to fit other special occasions as well!

Fran Tortorici—Three-Year-Olds
Castleton Hill Moravian Preschool
Staten Island, NY

## Colorful Kites

Welcome spring with these sun-catching kites. To make one, trace and cut out a kite shape from construction paper. Then cut the middle from the kite, leaving a frame. Attach the kite frame to the adhesive side of a piece of Con-Tact® covering; then trim around the frame to remove the excess. Place the kite on a table with the adhesive side facing up. Fill its middle with an assortment of small tissue-paper squares. Complete the project by adding a yarn tail. Tape the kites to your classroom windows for a great stained-glass look. Get ready; here comes a breeze!

Amy Jenkins—Preschool
Children's Country Day School
Mendota Heights, MN

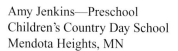

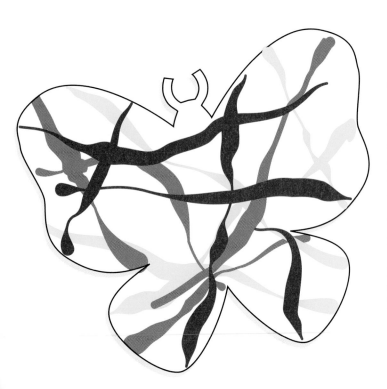

## Spread Your Wings!

Youngsters will be all aflutter over these beautiful butterflies. To prepare for this painting project, pour several different colors of tempera paint into individual Styrofoam® trays. Attach a clothespin to one end of each of three one-foot lengths of yarn. Holding a piece of yarn by the clothespin, dip it into a tray of paint; then drag it over a construction-paper butterfly shape. Repeat the process as desired with the same or different colors of paint. What a beautiful effect!

Louise Anderson—Four-Year-Olds
Community Cooperative Nursery School
Norwalk, CT

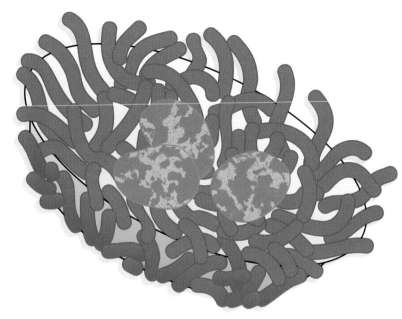

## Home Tweet Home

Any bird would love to claim this nest—complete with eggs—as its home! Mold egg shapes from Crayola® Model Magic™ modeling compound; then set the eggs aside for a day to dry. When the eggs have dried, sponge-paint each one for a speckled effect. To make a nest, paint glue on the inside of a small paper bowl. Press short lengths of brown yarn onto the bowl. Repeat the painting and pressing process on the outside of the bowl. When the nest and painted eggs are dry, place the eggs in their new home. Tweet! Tweet!

Linda Hilliard—Preschool
Child Care Centers
Arlington, VA

## Dazzling Dragonfly

Your little darlings will "ooh" and "ahh" over these winged wonders. Prepare dragonfly body and wings templates similar to the shapes shown. Trace and cut out the body from green construction paper and the wings from waxed paper. Sprinkle assorted colors of crayon shavings onto half of the wings shape. Fold over the other half; then press the wings with an iron set on low heat to melt the shavings. Add facial features to both sides of the dragonfly body; then fold it in half. Fold the wings in half again and insert them into the fold of the body. Staple all of the thicknesses together; then press the wings down onto the body. Punch a hole through the body and wings, insert yarn for hanging, and tie the ends. Bend the wings upward before hanging this dazzling dragonfly.

Jennifer Cresina—Preschool
Trinity Center For Children
Pottsville, PA

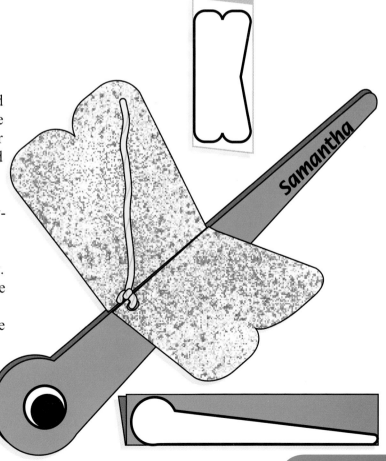

## Pussy Willows All Around

In preparation for this work of art, encourage children to carefully examine a real pussy-willow branch. Then provide sheets of light brown butcher paper, brown tempera paint, and thin paintbrushes. Instruct each child to paint several long, thin branches on her paper. (Or glue pipe cleaners to the paper to resemble branches.) Then provide white or off-white tempera paint. Have each child repeatedly dip a finger into the white paint, then onto her paper around the branches. When the paint dries, display each picture on a bulletin board around real pussy-willow branches.

Catherine V. Herber
Raleigh, NC

Anne M. Cromwell-Gapp—Gr. K
Connecticut Valley Child Care Center
Claremont, NH

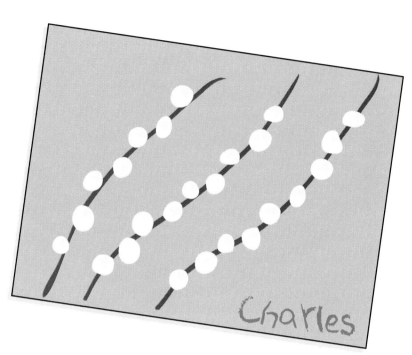

## Out On A Limb

These one-of-a-kind fliers will bring your youngsters to their feet! To make a footprint fowl, ask a child to remove a shoe and sock. Paint the bottom of his foot with washable liquid paint; then direct him to press his foot onto a sheet of construction paper. (Have a bucket of warm, soapy water and towels nearby for easy cleanup.) When the paint is dry, cut out the footprint. The child completes his project by gluing on real feather wings, a paper beak, and wiggle eyes. Display the projects among a tangle of paper vines and leaves.

Becky Brantley—Pre-K
Patterson Elementary School
Panama City, FL

## Rainbow Wand

Making a rainbow wand is not just an artistic endeavor—it will also be lots of fun to use outdoors! To make a wand, cut a large paper plate in half; then cut off the rim of the plate. Color arches on the plate to resemble a rainbow. Next cut one-inch-wide lengths of various colors of crepe-paper streamers. Staple the streamers to one end of the plate. Take the rainbow wand outdoors and as you move about, let the colors flap in the wind!

Linda Ann Lopienski
Asheboro, NC

## Springtime Robin

These robin redbreasts are sure to give your classroom a touch of spring. To make a robin, photocopy the patterns on page 107 on the appropriate colors of construction paper. Cut out the patterns. Then glue the breast cutout on the bird. Staple the wings to the back of the bird; then fold the wings upward. Add a construction-paper beak and marker details. Then attach a length of string or yarn to the bird. Suspend these sweet "tweeties" from your ceiling for a fine-feathered display.

Carol Hargett
Kinderhaus III Early Learning Center
Fairborn, OH

## Green-Haired Potato Heads

There's something about a potato head that just never goes out of style. So try this version with your youngsters to inspire lots of creativity, giggles, and grins. For each child, scoop out a well from the center of a potato—about one inch deep. Then provide markers, art supplies, cotton balls, a water-filled plant sprayer, and grass seed. To make one potato head, use the art supplies to create a face on the potato. Then loosely stuff cotton balls into the well. Spray the cotton with water; then generously sprinkle the grass seed on the cotton. Spray the cotton and seed again. Place the potatoes on a tray and set them in a sunny place. Each day, spray them with water. Within just a few days, your youngsters' potato heads will be sprouting green hair! Anybody need a haircut?

Jane Bray—Gr. K
Brooker Elementary
Brandon, FL

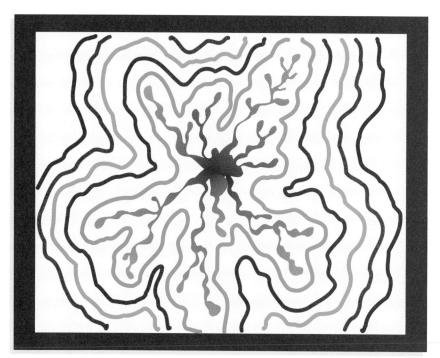

## Blow Art

The spring winds are beginning to blow—and so is the paint in your classroom! To make this windy-looking picture, drop a blob of thinned paint onto a sheet of art paper. Use a straw to blow the paint around until you have achieved a desired effect. When the paint is dry, use markers or crayons to repeatedly draw around the design. Mount each page on a colorful sheet of construction paper; then display the finished projects.

## Eggshell Rainbow

Looking for an interesting rainbow craft? If so, give this eggshell rainbow a try. In advance collect a supply of clean, dry, crushed eggshells. In each of several bowls, mix together two tablespoons of vinegar, a cup of hot water, and approximately ten drops of food coloring (using a different color for each bowl). Place some of the crushed eggshells in each bowl. Gently stir the eggshells until they absorb the desired amount of color. Spoon the eggshells onto paper towels and allow them to dry. To make a rainbow, use a paintbrush to spread glue in an arch shape onto a sheet of construction paper. Then sprinkle the eggshells onto the glue, using one color for each arch of the rainbow. Allow the glue to dry. To finish the project, glue cotton balls to each end of the rainbow to resemble clouds. Then brush an additional layer of diluted glue atop the eggshells. Now that's colorful!

Randalyn Larson
E. J. Memorial School
Jackson, MI

## Feet Aflutter

Step right into this tactile experience that results in a collection of one-of-a-kind butterflies. To make one butterfly, have each student step into a shallow pan of tempera paint with one bare foot, then press that paint-covered foot onto a sheet of construction paper. Repeat the process with the other foot as shown. When the footprints dry, cut loosely around them. Then cut out a construction-paper butterfly body and glue it between the two footprints. (If your youngsters' abilities permit, this is a great time to talk about left and right—and backwards!) For a colorful spring display, mount the completed butterflies around a construction-paper tree.

Melissa Mapes—Pre-K
Little People Land Preschool
St. Petersburg, FL

## Beautiful Butterflies

Brighten up your classroom with a bounty of these beautiful butterflies.

**For each one you will need:**

| | |
|---|---|
| 1/2 of an egg carton (six aligned cups) | water |
| | stapler |
| tempera paint | hot glue gun |
| 4 coffee filters | wiggle eyes |
| water-based markers | pipe cleaners |

**To make one:**

Paint the egg-carton half with tempera paint to resemble a butterfly's body; then let it dry. To decorate the coffee filters (wings), dip the markers into water and then "paint" the filters with the wet markers. (Dried-up markers work for this too!) When the wings are dry, staple each pair of wings together. Next use hot glue to attach them to the body. Add the finishing touches by gluing two wiggle eyes and pipe-cleaner antennae on one end of the egg carton. Hang these winged beauties from your ceiling.

Anita Boomgarden—Gr. K
Chatsworth Elementary
Chatsworth, IL

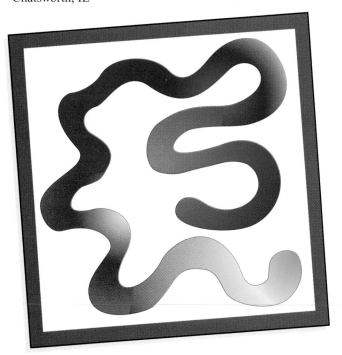

## Snazzy Designs

Using food coloring will get your budding artists' creative juices flowing and will get them thinking about the Easter activities soon to come. In advance, color several small bowls of water with different colors of food coloring. Provide a dropper (such as an eyedropper) for each different color of water. To begin the project, use glue to make a design on a square of white tagboard. While the glue is wet, sprinkle salt atop it. Then gently tip the square to allow the excess salt to slide off. Next squeeze different colors of food coloring onto the salt—***one drop at a time.*** (Youngsters will love watching the colors absorb into the salt!) Allow the glue to dry; then mount the design on a slightly larger square of colorful construction paper or tagboard. Mount the finished projects on a classroom wall or bulletin board for a snazzy springtime display.

Darlene Quinby
Calvary Episcopal School
Richmond, TX

## April Showers...

These radiant raindrops are sure to help bring about beautiful spring blossoms. To make one, cut a raindrop shape from blue construction paper; then trim away the center of the shape, leaving only a border. Press this border onto the adhesive side of a slightly larger piece of clear Con-Tact® covering. Press various shades of blue tissue-paper pieces on the covering. Trim around the edge of the raindrop. If desired, punch a hole near the center top of the drop and attach a length of clear thread for hanging. To create a downpour of compliments, hang the drops near a classroom window.

Amy Jenkins—Preschool
Children's Country Day School
Mendota Heights, MN

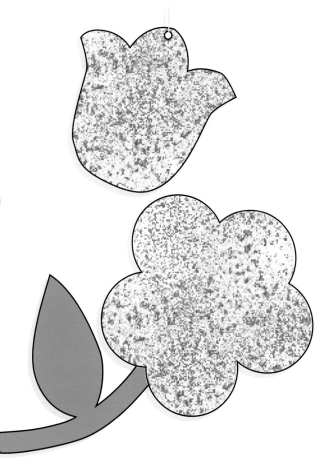

## ...Bring May Flowers!

Just as we promised, springtime showers will inspire a classroom full of these showy flowers. Using a wide-tip, permanent marker, trace a large flower shape onto a piece of waxed paper. Paint a layer of watered-down glue inside the entire shape. Sprinkle colorful paper or foil confetti over the shape; then drizzle another layer of glue over the confetti. Press a second sheet of waxed paper onto the glue-covered confetti. When the glue is dry, cut along the outline through all of the thicknesses. Punch a hole near the edge of the flower and attach a length of thread for hanging. Or add a paper stem to each flower and display them above windowsills to create the effect of a spring-time flower garden.

adapted from an idea by Pamela Vance—Preschool
Lake Geneva Cooperative Preschool
Lake Geneva, WI

### Peekaboo!

Peck, peck, peck. Cheerful chicks peek out of these decorated eggs. To make a peekaboo chick, cut two identically sized egg shapes from white construction paper. Decorate one egg shape with crayons or markers. Color the second egg shape yellow. Cut two white circles, two slightly smaller black circles, and an orange triangle from construction paper. Glue the shapes to the yellow shape as shown to create a chick. Cut the decorated egg in half to resemble a cracked egg. Tape both halves of the egg to the sides of the chick. If desired, add a holiday message. Peekaboo! Here's an Easter card for you!

Betsy Ruggiano—Three-Year-Olds
Featherbed Lane School
Clark, NJ

### A Sponge-Painted Bunny

A bit of sponge is what gives this fluffy-looking bunny its soft, furry look. To make one, use white chalk to trace or draw a rabbit shape onto a sheet of colored construction paper. Using a small sponge and white tempera paint, sponge-paint inside the entire rabbit outline. Allow the paint to dry; then use markers to add facial features and other decorative details. What a cute bunny!

Barbara Meyers—Gr. K
Fort Worth Country Day School
Fort Worth, TX

## Fancy Eggs

These fancy eggs will be a festive addition to any bulletin-board basket. To make one egg, trace or draw an egg on construction paper; then cut it out. Cut a doily in half; then cut out the middle section from the doily. Glue the outer edge of the doily on the egg cutout; then trim the excess around the egg. Using different colors of tempera paint, sponge-paint the design of your choice on the egg. When the paint dries, the eggs are ready for displaying. "Egg-ceptional"!

Betsy Chaplick—Gr. K
Indianapolis, IN

## Easter Bonnets And Top Hats

After your little ones make these bonnets and top hats, you'll want to plan to have an Easter parade! To make a bonnet, trace the top of a small, paper bowl onto the center of a paper plate. Cut a circle from the center of the plate that is slightly smaller than the resulting outline. Insert the bottom of the bowl through the hole; then staple the rim of the bowl to the plate. Paint the bonnet. When the paint is dry, embellish the bonnet with ribbon, lace, artificial flowers, netting, feathers, or small, decorative animals. Punch two holes opposite each other on the rim of the hat; then tie a length of curling ribbon through each hole.

To make a top hat, paint a small popcorn tub black. Cut a brim from black poster board; then staple it to the rim of the tub. Add pizzazz to the top hat by adding wide ribbon, large feathers, or small, decorative animals. Hats on, everyone? It's time for an Easter parade!

Cindi Zsittnik—Pre-K
Wesley Grove Pre-K
Hanover, MD

### Hens And Chicks

These hens and chicks are so adorable, even Old MacDonald would be proud! To make a hen, partially stuff a lunch-size paper bag with newspaper. Twist the remainder of the bag to create the hen's neck; then tie it with yarn. Staple the opening of the bag; then add crayon eyes and a construction-paper beak. Glue a supply of colorful feathers onto the paper-bag chicken.

To make a chick, purchase yellow cotton balls or tint cotton balls yellow by shaking them in a bag of yellow paint powder. To the cotton-ball chick, glue an orange construction-paper beak and black eyes that have been hole-punched from construction paper. Squirt a drop of glue in the bottom of a plastic Easter egg; then set the chick inside. Cluck, cluck!

Audrey Englehardt—Preschool Hearing Impaired
South Roxana School
South Roxana, IL

### Spring Basket

Fill this basket with decorative grass and eggs for a breath of springtime in your classroom. To make a basket, cut 2/3 off the top of a two-liter soda bottle. Discard the top portion of the bottle. Punch holes opposite each other near the rim of the bottle. Attach a long pipe cleaner from one hole to the other to form a handle. Then glue pastel-colored tissue-paper pieces on the bottle. When the glue dries, use puffy fabric paint to personalize the basket. When the paint dries, your basket is ready for filling!

Erlyne R. Osburn—Gr. K
Carousel School
Rancho Cordova, CA

## Magnificent Mélange

The striking appeal created here is entirely child-made! In advance make several tagboard egg tracers. To make one picture, trace an egg several times onto a sheet of white paper, overlapping the shapes as desired. Then use crayons (pressing hard) to outline and decorate the eggs. Paint over the entire paper with water-diluted black tempera paint. When the paint is dry, mount the artwork on a colorful construction-paper background. Display all of these projects along your classroom wall. Magnifique!

Carol Corby—Gr. K
St. Aloysius School
Jackson, NJ

## Barefoot Chicks

If you're having to scratch around for new craft ideas, you're going to get a big cluck out of these spring chicks! Ask a child to remove a shoe and sock; then paint the bottom of his foot with yellow washable liquid paint (giggling allowed!). Have him press his foot onto a sheet of construction paper. When the child's foot is clean and the paint is dry, have him use crayons to add an eye, beak, and legs to his chick. Finally have him spread glue along the bottom of the paper, then sprinkle the glue with cornmeal. Expect youngsters to chirp with delight when making these barefoot chicks!

Cindy Lawson—Three-Year-Olds
Educare Center
Fort Wayne, IN

### Just Hatched!

Have your youngsters craft these adorable duck-lings to create an endearing classroom display. For each child, duplicate the patterns on page 108 on white construction paper. To make one duckling, cut out the patterns. Lightly press a cotton ball into powdered, yellow tempera paint. Rub the cotton ball on the duck, redipping it in the powdered paint until the desired effect is achieved. Then use markers, crayons, and construction paper to add the duck's facial features. Glue the bottom and top shell pieces onto the duck. When each child has made a duckling, have him write his name on his bottom shell. Display all the projects in and around a large, bulletin-board paper nest titled "[Your name]'s Brood."

Cindy Pearson—Gr. K
Enoch Elementary
Cedar City, UT

### Her Favorite Cookbook

This collection of student-illustrated recipes is sure to become Mom's favorite cookbook! To make one for each child's mom, type or write on separate sheets of paper each recipe used in your class so far this year. Include snack recipes and recipes for dough, bubbles, or fingerpaint. Ask several children to illustrate each recipe. Program a title page with "Our Young Chefs"; then have each child print a thumbprint on the page. Write the child's name and add facial features to her thumbprint. Duplicate a title page and a set of recipes for each mother. To make each book, place a set of pages between construction-paper covers; then bind them. To decorate the cover of the book, have a child use yellow paint to put several thumbprints as shown on the sheet of paper. Then have him add white thumbprint petals around each yellow print to create daisies. When the paint is dry, use markers to add stems and a bow. Now that's a gift that's as useful as it is special!

Claudia Pinkston—Four-Year-Olds
Lexington United Methodist Preschool
Lexington, SC

## Mom's Greatest Fan

These Mother's Day greetings are sure to bring smiles to your children's moms. To begin, you'll need a large sheet of sturdy construction paper programmed with "I'm your biggest fan!" and a piece of wallpaper from a wallpaper sample book. (The wallpaper sample should be rectangular—approximately 9" x 18"—so that it will fan out nicely.) Accordion-fold the wallpaper; then staple it near one end of the folded paper. Gently spread out the wallpaper to create a fan shape. Tie a ribbon around the stapled end; then glue or staple the fan to the large sheet of construction paper. Write a Mother's Day message on the background paper; then it's ready for an extraspecial delivery!

Jennifer Hart—Grs. K–3
St. Paul's Lutheran School
Prior Lake, MN

## Mommy's Little Angel

Moms will be so appreciative of this gift that you and your little ones will end up wearing halos! Purchase a white, adult-sized T-shirt for each child's mother. Using fabric paint, generously paint a child's hand yellow. Have him press his hand onto the shirt to form the wings. After the child's hand has been washed and dried, paint it once more with a different color of his choice. Have him press his hand on the shirt again to form the body. Using the appropriate colors of fabric paint for each child, add a head, hair, eyes, and a mouth. Personalize the shirt and add the phrase "Mommy's Little Angel." If necessary, follow the manufacturer's instructions to permanently set the paint. When each shirt is complete, wrap it in paper that has been embellished with youngsters' handprints.

Lisa Bayer—Preschool
The Pre-Kindergarten Center of Woodhome, Inc.
Baltimore, MD

## Mother's Day Magnet

Moms will bloom with pride when they receive these child-crafted Mother's Day mementos. Have each child make one magnet for the special mother figure in his life. Then invite him to loosely wrap the flower in colorful tissue paper and tie a bow around the top. To Mom, with love!

**For each one you will need:**

craft foam
squeezable fabric paint
craft glue
green pipe cleaners
1 child's small, color photo
scissors
decorative craft scissors
(optional)
hot glue gun (optional)
self-adhesive magnetic tape

**To make one:**

Draw a flower on a sheet of craft foam; then cut it out. (Use decorative craft scissors to cut out the flower, if desired.) Glue your photo to the center of the flower; then decorate the flower with fabric paint, as desired. Next twist pipe cleaners together to make a stem and leaves. Using craft glue (or hot glue), attach the pipe-cleaner stem to the flower. Finally attach a strip of magnetic tape to the back of the flower.

Maureen Fredo
Ellis Johnson School
Laurinburg, NC

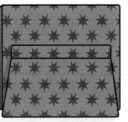

## Picture-Perfect

Here's a little treasure your students can make for Mother's Day, Father's Day, or any old day! In advance, take a picture of each of your students. Also ask youngsters to bring in empty, *cube-shaped* tissue boxes. To make one frame, cut off the top and bottom panels of a tissue box. Glue three sides of the top panel to the bottom panel, being sure that the design side is showing. If necessary, trim a photo; then slide it into the opening of the frame. To make a stand for the frame, cut out a piece that is approximately two-thirds the length of the frame from a side panel of the tissue box. Fold one edge of that piece one-half inch down. Glue the folded edge to the back of the frame. And there you go—picture-perfect!

Alyson Rappaport—Substitute Teacher
Gwinnett Schools
Stone Mountain, GA

Jackson Crane
May 6, 1999

A piece of me
I give to you.
I painted this flower
To say "I love you."

The heart is you,
The hand is me,
To show we are friends—
The best there can be.

I hope you will save it
And look back someday
At the flower we shared
On your special day.

—Kathleen Lademan

## Mother's Day Flower

Mothers will cherish these special flowers for years to come! In fact, you may want to suggest that these posy prints are perfect for framing. To make one, mount a sheet of white paper on a larger sheet of construction paper. Paint a child's palm a color chosen by the child, and his fingers a different chosen color. Have him press his hand onto the paper. When the paint is dry, glue a construction-paper stem and leaf cutouts below the flower. Glue a heart-shaped cutout to the center of the flower. Enlarge and duplicate the poem; then mount it below the print. Write, or have the child write, his name and the date. If desired make a card from the print by folding the paper in half and asking the child to write "Happy Mother's Day" on the outside of his card.

Kathleen Lademan—Pre-K
Noah's Ark Child Care Center
Portland, ME

## A Corsage For Mom

Moms will be delighted to wear these corsages on Mother's Day. To make one for a special lady, scrunch squares of tissue paper to resemble colorful blooms. Glue them onto the center of a small paper doily. Tape a safety pin to the back of the corsage. For you, Mom—here's a corsage as pretty as you are!

Kathi Michaud—Preschool
Little People Nursery School
Winslow, ME

### Pals Pillowcase

Saying good-bye at the end of a year spent with friends can be difficult. Cheer up your little ones by having each child make a school pals pillowcase. Provide a white, prewashed pillowcase for each student, or ask each child to bring one. Inside each child's pillowcase, place a personalized sheet of paper that is the length and width of the pillowcase. On one side of each pillowcase, use a permanent fabric marker to write the poem shown, replacing the school name with your school's name. Then have each child use fabric paint to make a handprint on each pal's pillowcase. Label each handprint with the fabric marker. To permanently set the prints before washing, follow the paint manufacturer's instructions. When sleeping on these keepsakes, youngsters are sure to have sweet dreams of their school pals.

Cathy Schmidt—Preschool
DePere Co-op Nursery School, Green Bay, WI

Todd
Dean
Sara
Stevie
Rico

Now I lay me down to sleep.
I'll count these hands instead of sheep.
And always remember the friends I made
When I was at DePere Nursery School.

Laurie
Jamal
Kate
Ashanti
Joey

Thank you for helping me grow! June 1999

### Thanks For Helping Me Grow

These floral favors make great thank-yous to adult volunteers who have helped your class throughout the year. Trace a flower pattern onto white poster board and cut it out. Ask a child to decorate the flower with markers, crayons, or paint; then attach her photo to the blossom's center. Program each flower with the phrase "Thank you for helping me grow!" and include the date. Then give each one to a special helper.

To present a bouquet, tape a straw to the back of each of several flowers. Press a ball of clay into a plastic cup; then press the straws in the clay around the sides of the cup. Place the cup in the center of a tissue-paper square. Wrap the paper upwards around the cup, and tie it at the base of the flowers with ribbon. Attach a tag with a message of appreciation.

Kitty Moufarrege—Three-Year-Olds
Foothill Progressive Montessori Preschool
La Canada, CA

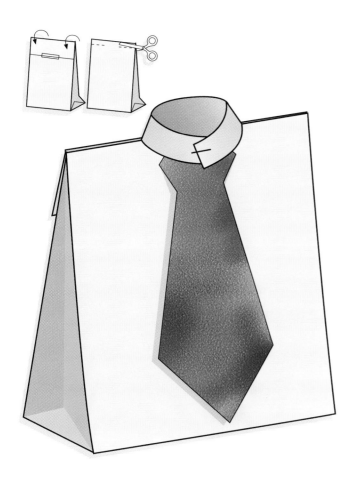

## Father's Day Gift Bag

Dad will love this one-of-a-kind designer shirt and tie! Place a Father's Day treat inside a white or colorful paper lunch bag. To transform the bag into a shirt and tie, fold down the top three inches. Tape the folded section to the bag. One inch below the fold, cut two inches toward the center of the bag on both sides. Bring the two top pieces toward the front of the bag to resemble the collar of a man's shirt. Staple the pieces together. To design a tie for Dad's shirt, use watercolors to paint a 6" x 3" piece of white construction paper. When the paint is dry, cut the paper to resemble a tie as shown. Glue the tie to the bag under the collar. Made especially for you, Dad—by me!

Dayle Timmons—Special Education Pre-K
Alimacani Elementary School
Jacksonville Beach, FL

## A Perfect Fit

Dads and Moms will absolutely love this gift idea to pieces. Remove the glass from a frame; then trace the outside and opening of the frame onto cardboard. Set the frame aside. Use an X-acto® knife to cut out the cardboard frame. Use tempera paint to paint the new frame and the desired number of puzzle pieces. When the paint is dry, glue the pieces to the frame. Print a message onto a tagboard strip; then glue it to the frame. Tape a photograph to the back of the frame. If desired, add magnetic tape to the back of the frame as well.

Donna Jennings—Special Education Preschool
United Cerebral Palsy Of New York City
Staten Island, NY

### Hold Everything!

Proud parents are sure to display these personalized pencil holders at work or at home. And as a bonus, each one is easy and inexpensive to make! Cut a light-colored piece of construction paper to match the height and diameter of a plastic container. (Powdered-drink containers work well.) Use crayons to decorate the paper. If desired, use craft glue to attach a school photo to the paper. Laminate the paper; then wrap it around the container and secure it with clear tape. Your little ones will present these gifts with love.

Kathy Doeing—Pre-K
St. Paul Preschool
Painesville, OH

### A Father's Day Magnet

No dad or caregiver will be able to resist this picture-perfect gift. In advance, photograph each of your students. To make one project, glue a photo to the center of a 6" x 6" square of sturdy cardboard. Have students glue colorful, scrunched-up, tissue-paper pieces on the cardboard to completely cover it. (You may want to do this in several sittings to ensure a thorough job.) When the glue dries, paint a coat of Mod Podge® over the picture frame. When that's completely dry, mount a piece of magnetic tape on the back. It's for you, Dad!

Seema Gersten
Harkham Hillel Hebrew Academy
Beverly Hills, CA

## Picture This, Dad!

Here's a frame Dad will be proud to display. To make a frame, glue eight craft sticks together in pairs; then set the sticks on waxed paper to dry. Glue the pairs together to form a frame. When the glue is dry, glue various types of pasta onto the frame. Again set the frame aside to dry. Brush on tempera paint or spray-paint the frame. When the paint is dry, spray the frame with acrylic finish. Attach a strip of self-adhesive magnetic tape to the back of the frame and it's ready for a pasta-perfect picture. Happy Father's Day!

Betsy Ruggiano—Three-Year-Olds
Featherbed Lane School
Clark, NJ

## Dad's Day Apron

Dads will treasure these Father's Day presents for years to come. In advance, purchase a classroom supply of simple, white aprons (found at most craft stores). Provide each child with an apron. Have each child paint one of his hands with fabric paint, then press his hand onto the apron. Have him continue in this manner until he is happy with his design. When the paint dries, ask each child why he loves his dad or male friend or relative. Use a fabric pen to write his response on the apron. This nifty apron will brighten up Dad's day!

Daphne M. Orenshein—Gr. K
Yavneh Hebrew Academy
Los Angeles, CA

## A Gift For Dad

This colorful, child-made paperweight takes some time to create, but the result is certainly worth it. A few weeks ahead of time, start collecting (and have children collect) envelopes that have canceled postage stamps on them. When you have a large supply of stamps for each child, have each child search his yard or your schoolyard for a rock. (You might want to give children size guidelines by comparing the size of the rock they should be looking for to a familiar object—such as a tennis ball.) To make one paperweight, wash the rock and let it dry. Cut the stamp(s) off each envelope, leaving a border of paper around each stamp. Soak the stamps in lukewarm water for ten minutes; then gently peel off each stamp. Arrange the stamps on waxed paper and let them dry. Then use white glue to glue the stamps on the rock, overlapping them to cover the rock completely. When the glue dries, paint on a coat of Mod Podge® (or any water-based sealer). When that dries, use a permanent marker to write your name on the bottom of the rock. Dads or other male friends will be thrilled to receive their youngsters' handiwork!

Maureen Tiedemann—Gr. K
Holy Child School, Old Westbury, NY

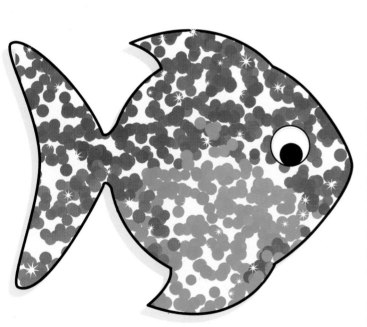

## Something's Fishy

The groovy technique used to paint these fish makes them look real enough to catch! Prepare a painting mitt for each different color of paint by folding a rectangular piece of bubble wrap in half, bubble side out, then stapling the sides. Put a mitt on one hand; then dip it into a shallow pan of paint. Press the mitt onto a large piece of white paper. Using a different mitt for each color of paint, paint the paper until it is covered. While the paint is wet, sprinkle on glitter. Cut a fish shape out of the paper when the paint is dry. Don't let this idea get away!

Pat Johnson—Three-Year-Olds
Church Of The Redeemer Preschool
Columbus, OH

## Sweet Starfish

Students will create star-quality starfish with this sweet painting technique. Combine sugar and several drops of food coloring with enough water to create a thick but paintable mixture. Use crayons to add features to a construction-paper starfish. Then paint the sugar mixture onto the starfish or spread the mixture on with your fingers. When the sugar mixture is dry, add these sweet starfish to a sand-and-surf display.

Joannie Netzler—Three-Year-Olds
A Special Place
San Jose, CA

## A Rock Lobster

This under-the-sea creature will really make a splash in your classroom. To make a rock lobster, cut off a row of three cardboard egg-carton cups. Paint the sections of the carton to resemble a lobster's body. When the paint dries, color and cut out a lobster tail and two claws. Glue the claw cutouts to one end of the lobster and the tail cutout to the other end. Then attach two pipe cleaners to resemble antennae. Glue two wiggle eyes to complete the lobster. Now this is a craft your little ones can put their claws on!

Ms. Guanipa—Gr. K
Covenant School
Arlington, MA

## Summary

## Creeping, Crawling Crabs

Red will be the color of the day when youngsters make these crafty crustaceans. To make one, fold a paper plate in half. Unfold the plate; then glue two sections of an egg carton onto one half of the outside of the plate as shown. When the glue is dry, paint the plate and the egg-carton sections red. When the paint is dry, refold the plate. Glue four red construction-paper strips to each side of the plate and glue wiggle eyes to the egg-carton sections. Which way to the beach?

Lesley J. Armstrong—Preschool
Sunrise Valley
Lawrence, KS

## Sandy Seashells

Children will love making sandy seashells to add to your beach or ocean studies. To make the shells, you will need your favorite hardening clay recipe, a rolling pin, an assortment of ocean-related cookie cutters, sandpaper, glue, paintbrushes, and play sand—regular or colored. To make one sandy sea-shell, roll out the dough to approximately 1/2-inch thick. Use a cookie cutter to cut out a shell shape; then let it dry for several days. When the shell is dry, gently sand it with sandpaper to make the surface rough enough for glue to stick to it. Next brush a coat of glue on the shell. Then roll the shell in the sand until it is covered. Display the dry project in your ocean-display area.

Bonnie McKenzie—Pre-K & Gr. K
Cheshire Country Day School
Cheshire, CT

## Outrageous Octopus

This craft idea for little hands makes an outrageous creature with oodles of arms. To make one octopus, open a brown paper lunch bag; then insert a forearm into the bag. Paint the outside of the bag purple. When the paint is dry, crumple a sheet of newspaper; then insert it into the bag. Use a rubber band to seal the bag just above the paper. Turn the bag upside down; then cut the portion below the rubber band into eight sections. Separate and twist each of the sections. Complete the tentacled creature by gluing on wiggle eyes. One, two, three, four, five, six, seven, eight! That octopus looks really great!

Jennifer Liptak—Three-Year-Olds
Building Blocks Of Learning
Denville, NJ

## Tropical Fish

These beautiful scenes of the tropics will grace your classroom with the cool, calming effects of an aquarium.

**To make one, you'll need:**

| | |
|---|---|
| white poster board | glue |
| 3 shades of blue fingerpaint, each mixed with glitter | pearls and sequins |
| | chenille pipe cleaners |
| play sand | shells (optional) |
| colorful fish cutouts | |

To make one, invite a child to use the sparkly fingerpaint to paint the entire surface of his poster board. When the paint is dry, have him use the rest of the supplies to create his own original tropical-water scene. If desired, punch holes near the top of the picture; then attach a length of ribbon for hanging. Listen...can't you just about hear the gentle waves?

Seema R. Gersten
Harkham Hillel Hebrew Academy
Beverly Hills, CA

## Bubble Fish

The fun is bubblin' over at this fishy art station!

**To prepare:**
1. Mix one cup of dishwashing liquid (Dawn® works well) with one gallon of water.
2. Pour this mixture into different-sized jars, filling each jar about half full.
3. To each jar, add a few drops of a different color of food coloring.

Give a child a sheet of white construction paper and a straw. Using the straw, have the child gently blow into one jar until the bubbles mound up over the rim. Then have him lay his paper on top of the jar for a few seconds. Encourage him to continue making bubble prints in the same manner, overlapping each print slightly. (Remind the child to rinse his straw with water before he uses a new color.) When the bubble prints are dry, have the child trace or draw a fish on his paper, then cut it out. Instruct him to use a permanent marker to add any desired fish details. To add the finishing touches, have the child brush a thin coat of water-diluted glue over the entire fish or just over certain places. Then have him lightly sprinkle glitter onto the diluted glue. When the glue dries, have the child shake off the excess glitter. Display these beautiful bubblers on a classroom board or wall.

Pamela Hernandez—Gr. K, Conway School, Escondido, CA

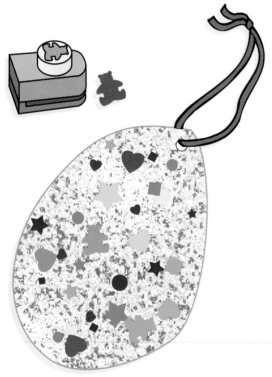

## Suncatchers

Look out! These suncatchers are really hot! Tape a long sheet of clear Con-Tact® covering (sticky side up) onto a tabletop. Provide students with craft materials such as foil pieces, glitter, sequins, confetti, tissue paper, and shaped hole punchers. Have each child use the punchers to create shapes from various types of paper. Have each child choose from the items and sprinkle the selected ones atop the Con-Tact® covering, decorating as much of the covering as possible. Then place another sheet of clear Con-Tact® covering, identical in size and shape, atop the first sheet. Gently press the pieces together.

To display this cooperative project, suspend the sheet from a window for a sparkling presentation. To make individual suncatchers, cut out desired shapes from the decorated sheet of Con-Tact® covering. Punch a hole at the top of each suncatcher. Thread a length of ribbon or yarn through the hole; then suspend each suncatcher from a window.

Paula M. Piraino—Four-Year-Olds
Trinity Pre-School
Topsfield, MA

## Mouthwatering Watermelon

You're going to want some watermelon seeds for this project, so why not give each student a wedge of real watermelon to get this project off to a tasty start. Ask students to save their watermelon seeds. Wash and dry the seeds before students begin their artwork. For this project, quarter several paper plates to create wedges. Provide two shades of green tissue-paper squares, and ask each student to glue some of these squares along the rim area of her wedge. Then provide two shades of red tissue-paper squares and have her glue them to cover the remaining area. To finish the watermelon wedges, have each student glue on several watermelon seeds. Yum!

## Buzzin' Bumblebees

Your little ones will be buzzin' to do this crafty activity. To make a bee, trace or draw a large bee shape on a double thickness of waxed paper; then cut on the resulting outline. Separate the bee cutouts. Sprinkle small amounts of yellow, black, and orange crayon shavings atop one bee cutout. Then place the other bee cutout atop the first one. Press a slightly warm iron on the bee; then lift the iron. (Do not slide the iron!) Repeat the process until all the crayon shavings have melted.

Barbara Pasley—Grs. K–1 Special Education
Energy Elementary
Energy, IL

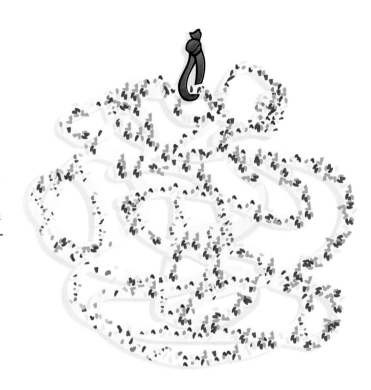

## Sand Squiggles

Decorate your classroom with these summery sand squiggles. To make one, squeeze a glue design on waxed paper, being sure that all the glue lines are thick and connected. Then sprinkle colored sand on the design. Let the project dry for approximately one week. When it is completely dry, gently peel the waxed paper from the design. Tie a loop of ribbon on the design so that it can be hung from a window, ceiling, or wall.

Anne M. Cromwell-Gapp—Gr. K
Connecticut Valley Child Care Center
Claremont, NH

## Snow Cones! Cotton Candy!

Come and get your summer treats right here, folks! To make a snow cone that will hold up in the hottest of weather, use tempera paint to paint half of a Styrofoam® ball. While the paint is wet, sprinkle the half-ball with clear glitter. Later press and glue it into a paper snow-cone holder.

For a cotton candy treat, paint a sheet of white construction paper with thinned glue; then stretch cotton balls and press them onto the paper. When the glue is dry, cut around the shape of the cotton. Spray-paint the cotton with thinned tempera paint. When the paint is dry, glue the cotton candy to a paper cone shape. The summer sun won't melt the fun of these terrific treats!

Charlet Keller—Preschool
ICC Preschool
Violet Hill, AR

## Creative Castles

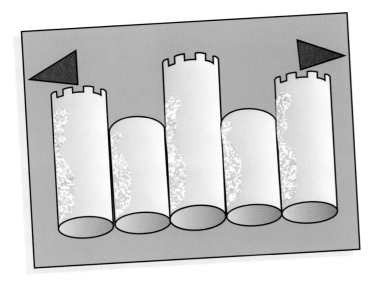

Here's a castle craft that encourages creativity. Cut a quantity of cardboard tubes into various lengths, cutting the tops of some to resemble a castle's towers. Encourage each child to manipulate and build with the tubes. Then provide him with a sheet of sturdy paper and a small tray of glue. To make a castle, a child dips a side of each of the tubes of his choice into the glue and arranges them on his paper. When the glue is dry, he then paints the castle gray. Or, to duplicate the look of a sand castle, have him paint the tubes yellow, then sprinkle the wet paint with a mixture of sand and glitter. Complete the castle with paper flags. To develop cooperation as well as creativity, try this craft idea as a small-group project. What stunning structures!

Kathleen Soman—Preschool
Wee Wisdom Preschool
New Port Richey, FL

## Desert Cactus

If you're studying the desert or if you're looking for a summer-related activity, here's the perfect craft for you. To make one cactus, trace or draw a cactus pattern on construction paper; then cut it out. Paint a coat of glue over the cutout. While the glue is still wet, sprinkle on parsley flakes until the whole cactus is covered. When the glue dries, shake off the excess parsley. These cacti look great on a classroom desert mural.

Rachelle Thompson—Gr. TK
Paxton Child Development Center, Leesburg, VA

## Handprint Sunflowers

Little ones will love this sunflower project hands down! To prepare, mix together yellow tempera paint and a few drops of liquid soap in a shallow pan. To make a sunflower, paint a brown circle near the top of a large sheet of construction paper. Next repeatedly press one hand into the yellow paint, then onto the paper around the brown circle. When the paint dries, glue sunflower seeds to the center of the flower. Draw a stem and leaves on green construction paper; then cut them out. To complete the project, glue the stem and leaves on the paper under the handprints. What beautiful blooms!

adapted from an idea by Cindy Larson—K–2 Special Education
Western Hills Elementary
Omaha, NE

## Super Suncatchers

Catch some rays with these super suncatchers. Before beginning this project, prepare a sun-shaped template. Using a permanent marker, trace the template onto a sheet of waxed paper. Paint slightly watered-down glue over the resulting sun shape; then cover the entire area with yellow and orange tissue-paper squares. Carefully apply additional glue over the tissue paper. Press another sheet of waxed paper atop the glue-covered tissue paper. When the glue is completely dry, cut a sun shape by cutting through all thicknesses along the marker outline. Give the suncatcher personality by adding marker and foam-piece facial features. Punch a hole near the top of the suncatcher and thread with a length of yarn; then suspend it near a window. Let the sun shine!

Pamela Vance—Preschool
Lake Geneva Cooperative Preschool
Lake Geneva, WI

## Firecracker, Firecracker!

Boom, boom, boom! These dazzling fireworks explode with color and sparkle! To create a fireworks display, prepare several colors of tempera paint so that the paint is of a thick consistency. Add ultrafine glitter to the paint. Randomly put several drops of each different color of paint on a sheet of black construction paper. Using cotton swabs, spread the paint away from the drops so that they resemble fireworks. As a finishing touch, sprinkle multicolored glitter over the wet paint. Display these fantastic works together and you're sure to set off a big bang of compliments!

Gayle Simoneaux, Linda Powell, and Ellen Knight—Four-Year-Olds
Pineville Park WEE
Pineville, LA

## Bursting In Air!

Colorful fireworks will be bursting all over your classroom when your youngsters get their creative hands working on these projects.

**You will need:**
empty film canisters
foam pieces (cut to fit inside the canisters)
pipe cleaners
magnetic tape
pencils
glitter glue

First instruct a child to attach a piece of magnetic tape to a film canister. Then invite her to use the glitter glue to decorate the canister. When the glue is dry, have her stuff a piece of foam into the canister. Show the child how to curl pipe cleaners by wrapping them around a pencil. Or she could bend and twist the pipe cleaners as desired. Have her insert one end of each pipe cleaner into the foam. Display all the finished projects on magnetic surfaces around your classroom.

Marjorie Watson—Gr. K
Apalachin Elementary School
Apalachin, NY

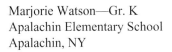

### Blast Off!

Assist your aspiring astronauts as they make these rockets. To make one, paint a small cardboard tube. When the paint is dry, cut four slits equal distances apart on one end of the tube. Decorate the tube with patriotic and star-shaped stickers. Cut two equilateral triangles from construction paper. Cut a slit in one triangle from its base to its center and a slit in the other triangle from its tip to its center. Fit the triangles together; then slide the triangles into the slits of the cardboard tube. Cut away one-third of a paper circle as shown; then reshape the paper into a cone and tape the ends together. Glue the cone to the top of the rocket. 10, 9, 8,…we have liftoff!

Cheryl Cicioni—Preschool
Kindernook Preschool
Lancaster, PA

### Star-Spangled Fun

Oh, my stars! These projects will decorate your room with patriotic pizzazz! Using graduated sizes of star-shaped cookie cutters or different sizes of star templates, trace and cut out a supply of stars from foil; tagboard; and red, white, and blue construction paper. Select a variety of cutouts and sequence them by size; then arrange and glue them onto a flattened white paper plate. Glue layers of foil and construction-paper stars onto some of the tagboard stars; then punch a hole in each set. Punch one hole on one side of the plate and as many holes as there are tagboard stars on the opposite side of the plate. Tie the stars to the plate with lengths of curling ribbon; then thread the last hole with ribbon for hanging. Hang these projects in your room, and everyone is sure to be starstruck!

Lorrie Hartnett—Pre-K
Canyon Lake, TX

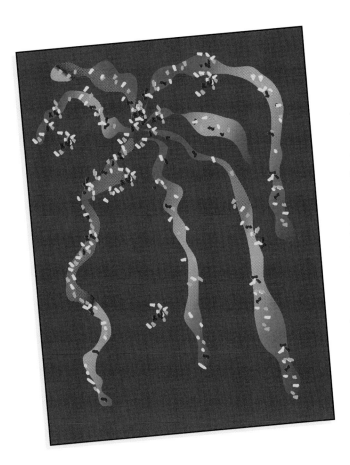

## Fireworks!

Help your youngsters celebrate Independence Day with these artistic creations. To begin, give each child a sheet of black construction paper. Then have each child dip a brush into white glue and paint a firework design on his paper. While the glue is still wet, have each child shake cake-decorating sugar sprinkles onto the glue. Let it dry; then shake off the excess sprinkles. As a variation, have a child place a handful of colorful candy sprinkles on the paper first. Then have him dip the brush into the glue and brush over the candy sprinkles. Oooh! Did you see *that* one?

Adapted from an idea by Anne M. Cromwell-Gapp—Gr. K
Connecticut Valley Child Care Center
Claremont, NH

## Firecracker Party Favors

Your little ones can make these party favors to decorate your classroom or to give away. For each child, you will need two small paper cups; red and blue tempera paints; scissors; red, white, and blue crepe-paper streamers; a paintbrush; and glue. To make one party favor, cut eight equally spaced slits down the side of one cup, stopping at the bottom rim. Cut the other cup in a similar fashion, but stop 1/2 inch above the bottom rim. Bend the cut pieces down, forming an open, flowerlike shape. Paint the cups; then let them dry. Next glue the shallower-cut cup inside the deep-cut cup. Cut thin streamers from crepe paper; then glue them to the back of the bottom cup. When the glue dries, fill the center with candies—red, white, and blue jelly beans would be nice!

Karen Eiben and Amy Gray—Gr. K
The Kids' Place
LaSalle, IL

Bottom Cup

Top Cup

## Soft-Touch Phone

Use a soft touch to help each student memorize her phone number and to learn her number's pattern on a phone keypad. For each child, duplicate the phone and receiver patterns (pages 109 and 110) on construction paper. For each child's phone, cut out a set of ten sponge squares. Label each sponge square with a different numeral from zero to nine. Invite each child to color her phone as desired, then cut it out. Help her arrange and glue the sponge buttons on her phone. Write the child's phone number on the back of her receiver; then attach the receiver to the phone with a length of curling ribbon. Have each child practice dialing her phone number, using the number on the receiver as a guide. Does she notice that she follows the same pattern each time she dials her number? After a few practice rounds, challenge her to dial her number from memory, referring to the receiver only if needed. For phone memory skills, the soft touch is the right touch!

Sandy Blumstein
Paley Day Care Center
Philadelphia, PA

## Happy Birthday To You!

Help children learn their birthdays while decorating these creative cakes. In advance, prepare cake-shaped templates. Trace a template on brightly colored tagboard; then cut on the resulting outline. Program the cake cutout with a name and birthday. Embellish the cake using a variety of art supplies such as yarn, colored glue, small decorating candies, and real candles. Consider using the completed projects to create a birthday graph or wall display.

## Hooray For Party Hats...

There's sure to be a party atmosphere in your classroom when youngsters create these zany party hats! Prepare several different colors of glue by adding tempera paint to bottles of white glue. To make a hat, embellish the underside of a paper bowl using the glue and a variety of art supplies such as glitter, feathers, and pom-poms. When the glue is dry, punch two holes on opposite sides of the bowl's rim. Tie a length of curling ribbon through both holes. There you have it. A ready-to-wear happy birthday hat!

Carrie Lacher
Friday Harbor, WA

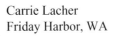

## ...And Horns!

Have more party fun with these festive noisemakers. Using markers and stickers, decorate a cardboard tube. Punch a hole about one inch from the bottom of the tube. Wrap a five-inch square of waxed paper around the tube's opposite end. Secure the paper with a rubber band. When everyone has made a party horn, put on some irresistible music. Then invite youngsters to march and toot to a birthday beat.

Carrie Lacher
Friday Harbor, WA

## Some Mighty Fine Swine

Your little ones will be hog-wild about these precious piggy projects! To make one, sponge-paint one side of two large paper plates and one small paper plate pink. When the paint is dry, poke a brad through the center of the smaller plate; then loosely attach this plate to one of the larger plates. Cut out and glue construction-paper ears, eyes, and a snout to the smaller plate. Staple the rims of the large plates together so that the unpainted sides face each other. Stuff the body of the pig with crumpled tissue paper. As a final touch, cut a tail from a pink construction-paper circle as shown; then glue the tail to the back of the pig. Very fine!

Lisa Scaglione—Four- And Five-Year-Olds
Children's Village Preschool
Sherrill's Ford, NC

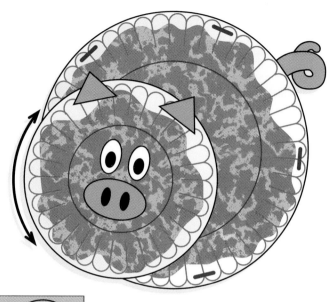

## Good "Moos"

Have you "herd" the good news? Making these "moos" strengthens fine-motor skills! Trace a cow pattern onto a sheet of white construction paper. Tear brown or black construction-paper spots; then glue the spots onto the cow. Add a button or wiggle eye. When the glue is dry, cut out the cow shape. Send these cows out to pasture by mounting them on a green background.

Amy Kapsis—Three- And Four-Year-Olds With Special Needs
Marathon Childhood Center
Middle Village, NY

## Fantastic Frames

Recycle old greeting cards to make these fantastic frames. To make a frame, cut off the front cover from an old greeting card. Then cut out the middle of the card, leaving a border that resembles a frame. (Cards that have border art work especially well.) Glue a child's artwork—one that is similar in size—to the back of the frame. Mount various framed masterpieces on a wall or bulletin board to make a classroom art gallery.

Tracey J. Quezada—Gr. K
Presentation Of Mary Academy
Hudson, NH

## Handy Magnets

Make handy magnet clips for holding student artwork. Begin by tracing a child's hand on tagboard; then cut out the shape. Label the cutout with the child's name or a cute phrase such as "Little Artist." Have each child decorate his hand cutout with an assortment of art supplies such as markers, glitter, and sequins. Onto the back of each decorated hand, glue a clothespin to which a magnet has been attached. When the glue is dry, the magnet clips can be sent home for each family's refrigerator art gallery. This craft is sure to be a hands-down favorite of parents.

Elizabeth Lyons—Gr. K
Tomahawk Elementary School
Lynchburg, VA

Little Artist

### Art Basics

Introduce youngsters to the work of the Dutch painter Piet Mondrian, and you've set the groundwork to reinforce *primary colors, shapes,* and lots of *creativity.* For inspiration, display pictures of Mondrian's work (such as those found in art-history books). Guide the discussion so children realize that Mondrian often used only the primary colors, black, and white. Then give each child a sheet of white poster board. Have each child create black shape outlines by gluing black construction-paper strips onto his poster board. Next have him paint the inside of each shape with a primary tempera-paint color—red, yellow, or blue—or white. During group time, invite each child to tell about the shapes and colors of his painting. Then display the paintings with the title "Our Masterpieces." Your gallery of geometric art is sure to attract lots of complimentary comments—and a chance for your youngsters to show off that they know about Piet Mondrian!

Marianne Cerra—Gr. K Enrichment Program
Family Growth Day Care, Nursery School, & Kindergarten
Shillington, PA

### Lovely Leis

This project is just perfect for keeping or for giving away. To make a lei, cut apart the cups of an egg carton. Encourage a child to paint his cups to resemble flowers, then embellish each cup with art supplies, such as glitter glue, pipe cleaners, beads, buttons, and tissue paper. Help the child poke a hole in the bottom of each cup. Then have him string the flowers using a plastic needle threaded with yarn. Encourage each child to wear his lei or give it away to a special person.

Lara Renfroe—Gr. K
Heber Springs Elementary School
Heber Springs, AR

## Magic Paint

The surprise at the end of this art project is that you've created a rainbow of color! Paint liquid starch onto a piece of art paper. Dip a damp paintbrush into powdered paint; then dab it onto the wet paper. The starch will change the powder into a thick paint. Repeat the process with other colors of powdered tempera to make a colorful design.

## Zany Zebras

Add zest to your craft time with these zebra projects. Cut a zebra shape from white construction paper. Place the zebra flat in a box's lid or plastic container. Place a paddleball in a spoon. Dip the ball into any color of paint; then drop the ball in the lid or container. Tilt the lid or container back and forth so that the ball rolls painted lines onto the zebra. Fringe a length of paper that matches the color of the paint. When the paint on the zebra is dry, glue the paper to the back of the zebra to resemble its mane.

Beverly Sandberg, Peace Lutheran Preschool, Palm Bay, FL

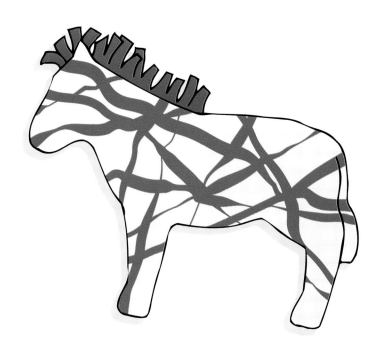

### Smile Like A Crocodile!

Wrap up a reptile unit with these snappy swamp lovers. To make one, place a plastic strawberry basket in the center of a sheet of green tissue paper; then wrap the paper upwards, tucking the ends in the basket. Glue two green pom-poms to the top of the basket; then glue wiggle eyes to the pom-poms. Cut apart the top and bottom sections of a cardboard egg carton. Cut off the flap from the bottom half of the carton. Paint both sections green. When the paint is dry, insert the sections into the basket as shown. Display the smiling crocodiles on a paper pond. Snap!

Abi Reiffman—Two-, Three-, And Four-Year-Olds
Yavneh Hebrew Academy
Los Angeles, CA

### Baking Dough

Your students will enjoy creating dough designs for jewelry, refrigerator magnets, or other decorations. They'll also love the fact that they can measure and mix the dough recipe on their own. Have each student mix and knead 4 tablespoons of flour, 1 tablespoon of salt, and 2 tablespoons of water. Have him roll the dough flat with a rolling pin, then use a cookie cutter or his hands to create his own dough designs. Bake the dough at 350° for 1 to 1 1/2 hours. Now that's a recipe for creativity!

Bonnie Pinkerton, Rockfield Elementary, Bowling Green, KY

Teresa

## I Love Your Funny Face

Everyone has eyes, a nose, and a mouth. But my—how different we all look! Be prepared for giggles when youngsters create these funny faces. In advance cut out magazine pictures of facial features. Label each of three containers with the name and a picture of a feature. Sort the pictures into the containers. Cut face shapes from various colors of skin-toned construction paper. To make a funny face, have each child select a face shape and two eyes, a nose, and a mouth from the magazine cutouts. Have him glue the face shape on a piece of paper and then glue the features on the face shape. Direct him to add hair to the face using markers or crayons. Let's face it—everybody's craft will be one-of-a-kind!

Doris Porter—Preschool
Headstart
Anamosa, IA

## A Colorful Creation

Youngsters will love this colorful idea. To prepare for this activity, place a classroom supply of red, yellow, and blue crepe-paper strips on a table. Have each child choose two differently colored strips, then place his strips in a glass jar. Assist each student in pouring water in the jar; then have him twist a lid on the jar. Encourage each child to carefully shake his jar and watch a secondary color appear. Place the jars on the center of a table and seat youngsters around the table. Then supply each child with a sheet of light-colored construction paper and a paintbrush. Encourage him to dip the paintbrush into the jar or jars of his choice, then to paint, drip, or splatter a picture or design.

Connie Allen
Immanuel Lutheran
Manitowoc, WI

## Turtle Time

These turtles will suit your little ones to a T. Sponge-paint a paper-plate half the colors of your choice. From green construction paper, cut a turtle head, a tail, and two legs. Glue the paper pieces to the back of the painted plate. Add a wiggle eye to the turtle's head to complete the project. Top off your turtle time by reading aloud any of the tales about Franklin the turtle by Paulette Bourgeois (all Franklin titles published by Scholastic Inc.).

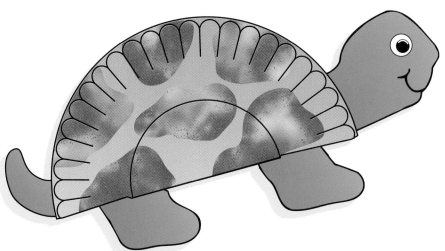

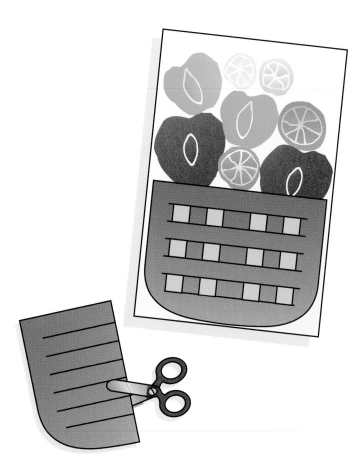

## Fantastic Fruit Basket

Here's a fresh art idea—weave a paper basket; then use real fruit to make tasty prints! To make the basket, fold a 9" x 12" sheet of construction paper in half. Cut a basket shape. Then cut slits in the basket one inch apart, stopping one inch from the outer rim of the basket. Weave one-inch-wide construction-paper strips through the slits. Trim, adjust, and glue the strips. Glue the basket to a 12" x 18" piece of construction paper. Cut an assortment of fresh fruit in half. Then dip the fruit in appropriate colors of paint and press the fruit onto the paper. Fruit, anyone?

Carmen Carpenter—Pre-K
Highland Preschool
Raleigh, NC

## Spaghetti Art

This activity sure has oodles of noodles. Provide each child with a sheet of waxed paper and some cooked spaghetti noodles. Have him arrange the spaghetti on the waxed paper in the design of his choice. Allow the pasta to harden a few days. To complete the project, have each student glue his design on colored oaktag. To vary this activity, use differently colored and shaped pasta. A perfectly fun pasta project!

Linda Anne Lopienski
Asheboro, NC

## Native American Bags

If your class is studying historic Native Americans, this craft fits right in. Explain to students that, long ago, many Native American men carried decorated bags made from deer or buffalo skin. After showing a variety of photographs of these bags, give each child the opportunity to make a decorated bag. To make one bag, cut off the bottom of a lunch bag. Cut fringe from the bag scraps; then glue or staple it to the bottom of the bag, also sealing the bottom of the bag. Then use markers or paint to decorate the bag as desired. Punch two holes in the top of the bag; then tie on a length of yarn to make a strap.

Debbie Hodges—Gr. K
Rockbridge Elementary
Norcross, GA

### Critter Cages

Your youngsters will be wild about this zoo-animals project. To make a cage for a critter, accordian-fold a black piece of construction paper. Cut an *I* shape out of the paper as shown; then unfold. Using construction-paper scraps and other art materials, make a zoo animal for the cage; then glue the animal to a white piece of paper. Glue the top and bottom of the cage cutout to the background page. What a zoo!

Tammy Bruhn
Little Farm School
Ypsilanti, MI

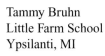

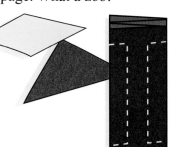

### Coffee Bears

This project is not only fun to make, but it is also a really sensory experience. To make a coffee bear, trace a bear pattern (or draw one yourself) on a sheet of brown construction paper; then cut on the resulting outline. Draw facial features on the bear. Next spread glue on portions of the bear to represent its stomach, ears, and paws. Then sprinkle dried coffee grounds atop the glue. When the glue dries, shake off the excess coffee grounds.

Sara Bockover—Gr. K
Keith Country Day School
Rockford, IL

## Fabulous Frames

These easy-to-make frames are sure to please! For each child, purchase or cut from tagboard a 5" x 7" mat that has a 3 1/2" x 5" opening for a photo. To decorate a frame, squeeze colored glue around the edge of the mat. When the glue is dry, tape a photo to the back of the frame. Send these unique frames home as gifts any time of the year.

Mary E. Maurer
Caddo, OK

## Underwater World

Here's an underwater art project that will really make a splash. To make a fishbowl and underwater scene, draw a fishbowl pattern on a sheet of construction paper; then cut it out. Use permanent markers and crayons to draw underwater pictures such as fish, seaweed, coral, and aquarium rocks. Mix a few drops of water and blue food coloring with some white glue. Then brush over the entire fishbowl with the blue mixture. Allow it to dry. There you have it—an underwater art experience.

Melissa L. Mapes
Little People Land Preschool
St. Petersburg, FL

### Handsome Lions

These child-made lions are rip-roarin' fun to make. Draw or paint a lion's face on a paper plate. Use other art supplies (such as pompoms, pipe cleaners, and buttons) to embellish the lion's face. Then—in several sittings, if appropriate—trace your hand a dozen or so times. Cut out the hand shapes; then glue them around the lion's face to resemble his mane. Curl the ends of the mane by wrapping the fingertips around a pencil and releasing. Glue on construction-paper ears for a "gr-r-r-r-eat" finish.

Sherry Cook—Preschool & Gr. K
Glenwood Springs, CO

### Chalk It Up!

Combine your students' artwork, stencils, and paper plates to create these rounded masterpieces. Soak large sticks of colored chalk in liquid starch for a few minutes. (Soaking time will vary depending on how porous your chalk is.) Using the chalk, have each student color in random fashion on heavily textured art paper. Allow the artwork to dry and weight it down to flatten it. Trace a stencil or template of each student's choice onto a thin paper plate. Use an X-acto® knife to cut on the resulting outline for each child. Have each student put glue on the rim of his paper plate, before turning it upside down onto the dried chalk artwork. When the glue is dry, have each student cut the excess paper from around the rim of his plate. If desired, have each student use colored glue to decorate his plate.

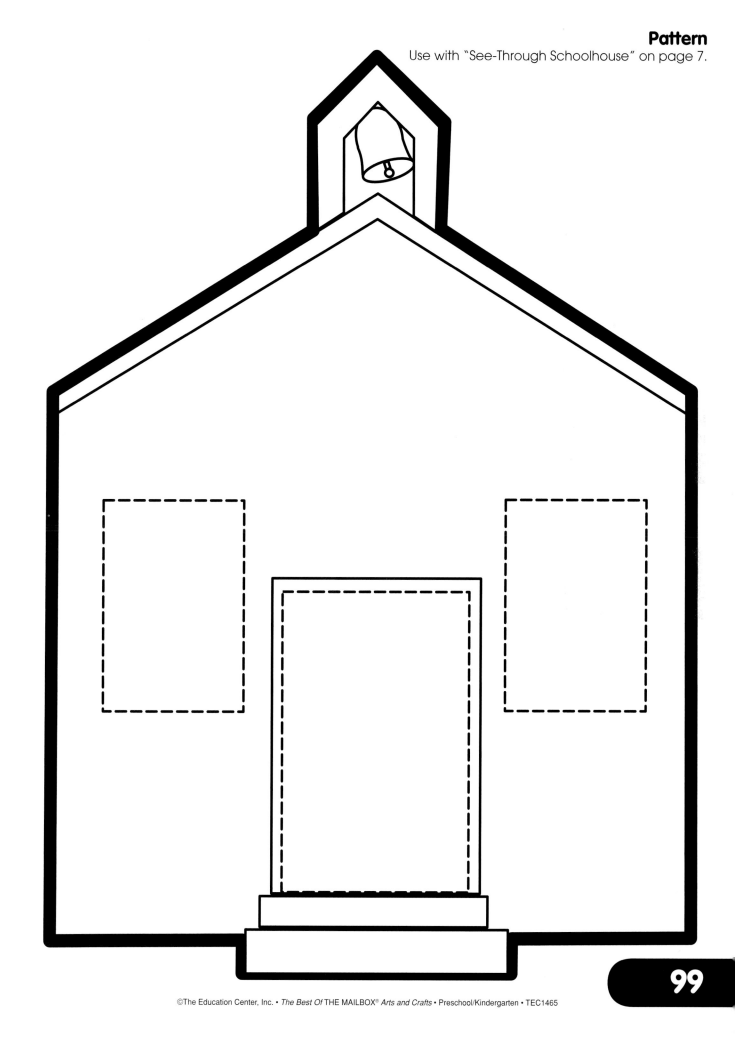

**Patterns**

Use with "Indian Corn" on page 20 and "A Crop Of Corn" on page 21.

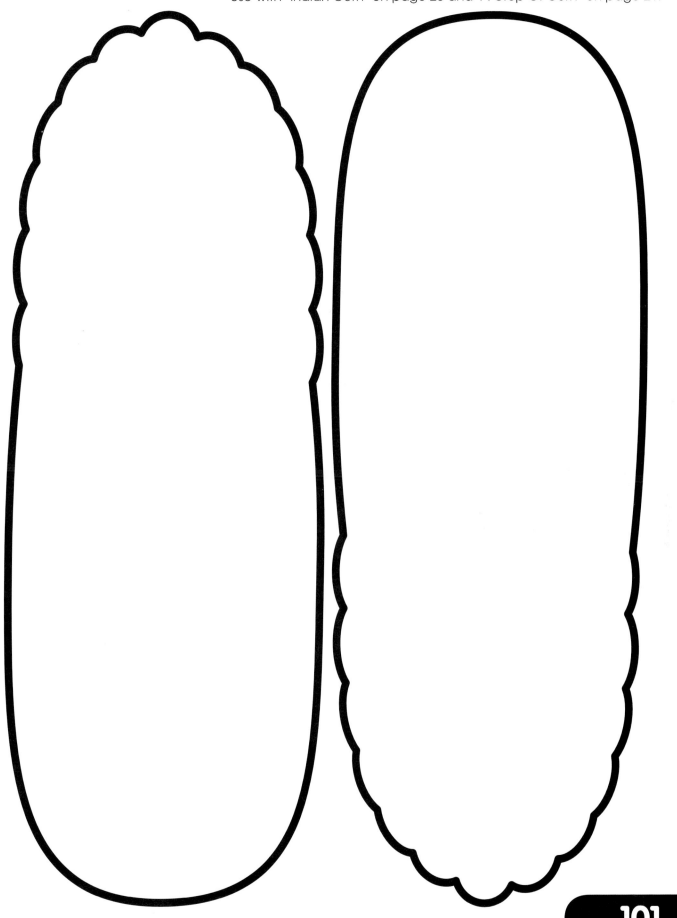

## Poem

Use with "Fingerprint Turkeys" on page 23.

All turkey birds are different,
From sea to shining sea.
And you'll never see another bird
Like this one to you from me.
Can you see what makes him different?
Do you need some helpful hints?
I made him from my very own
Thumb and fingerprints!

—Marsha A. Burks

## Patterns

Use with "Terrific Turkeys" on page 23.

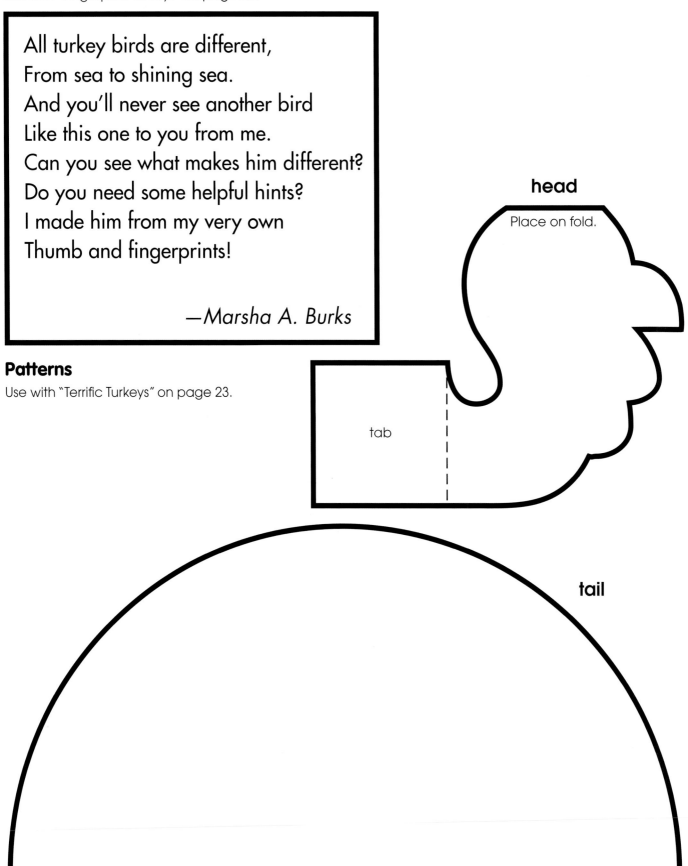

head

Place on fold.

tab

tail

102

**Pattern**
Use with " 'Scent-sational'
Gingerbread Folk" on page 30.

**Pattern**
**103**

## Patterns
Use with "Darling Dove Decorations" on page 40.

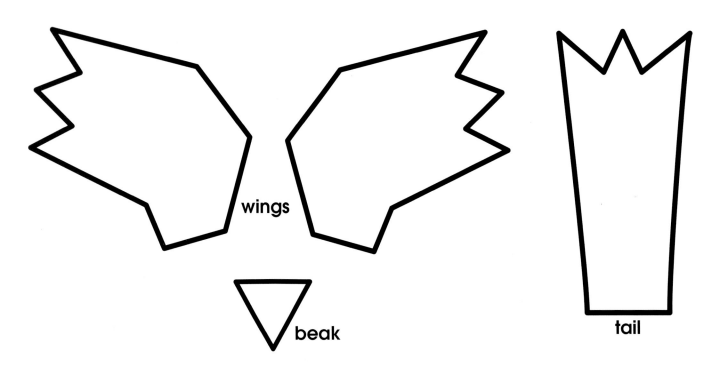

wings

beak

tail

## Patterns
Use with "Living In Harmony" on page 44.

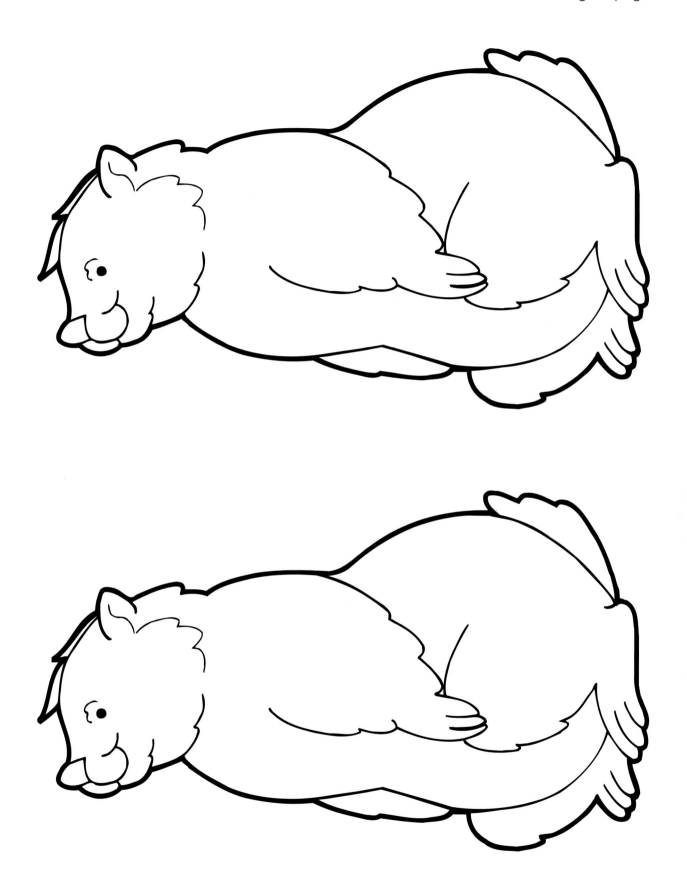

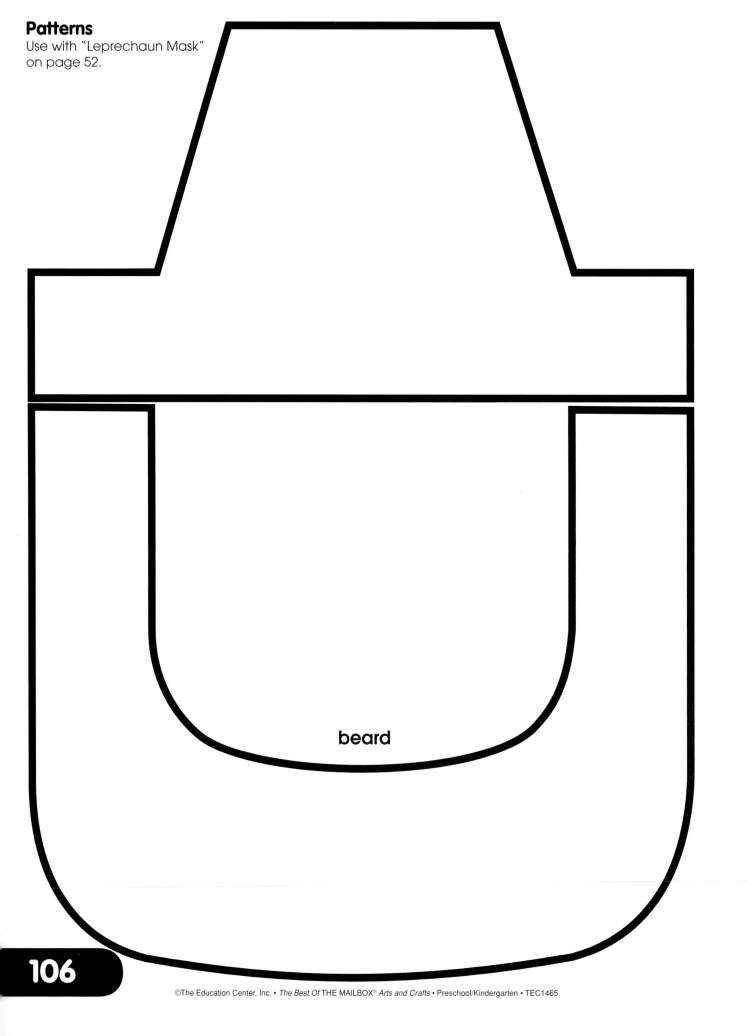

beard

**Finished Sample**

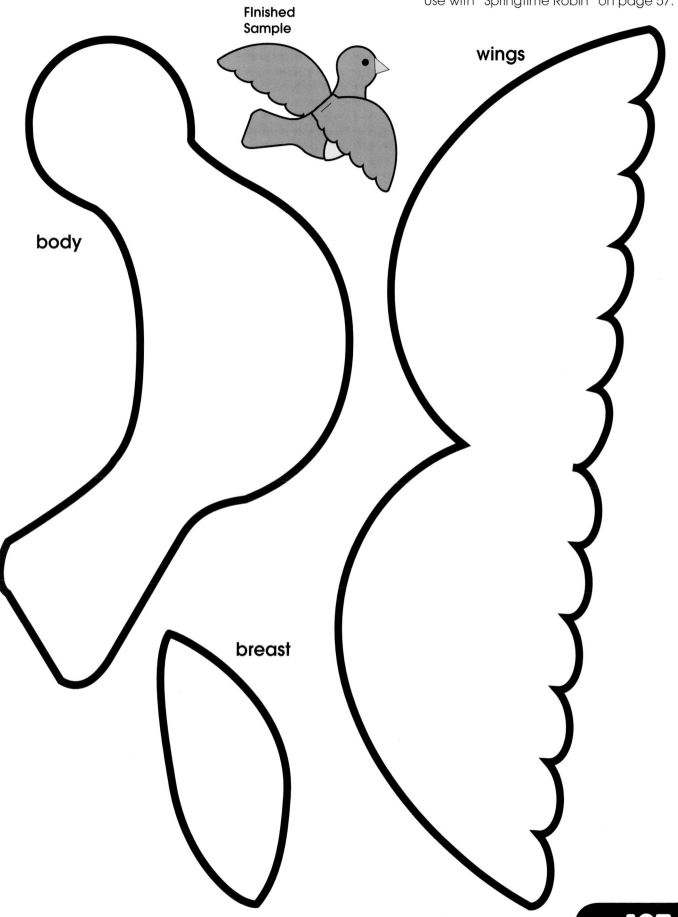

body

wings

breast

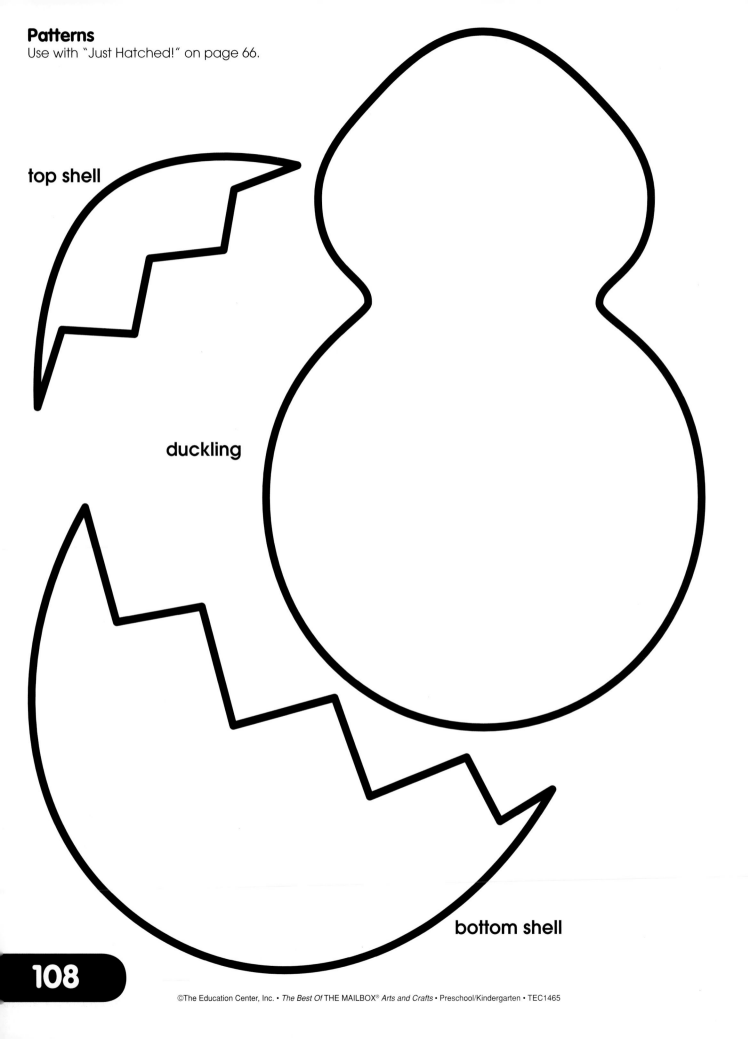

top shell

duckling

bottom shell

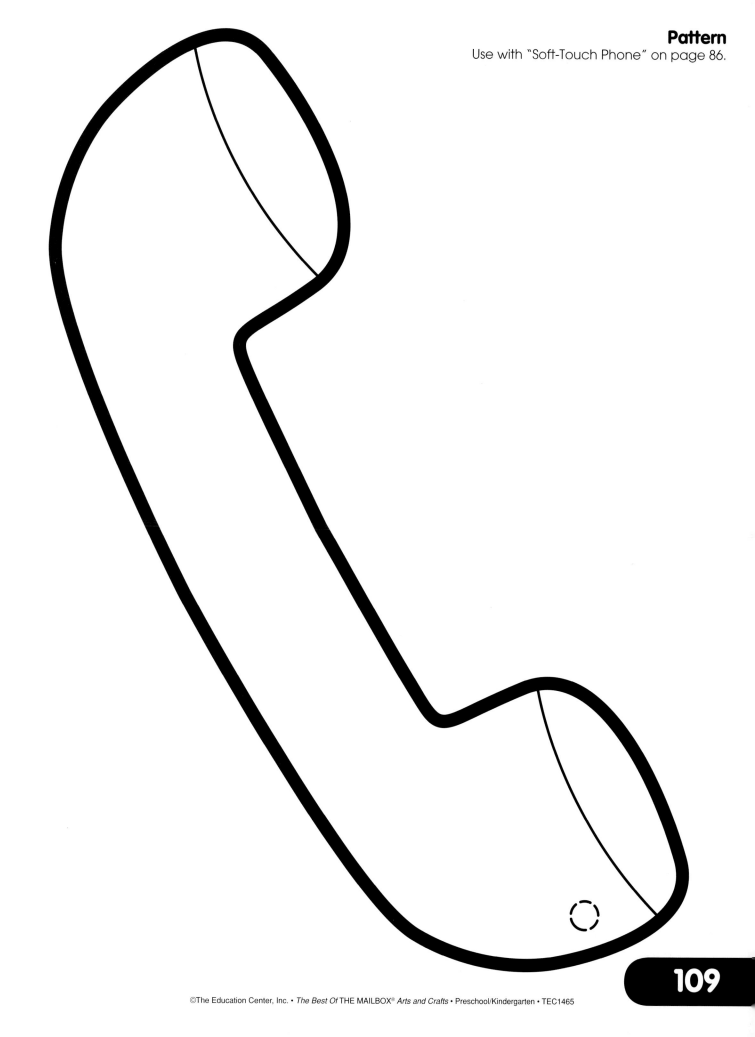

**109**

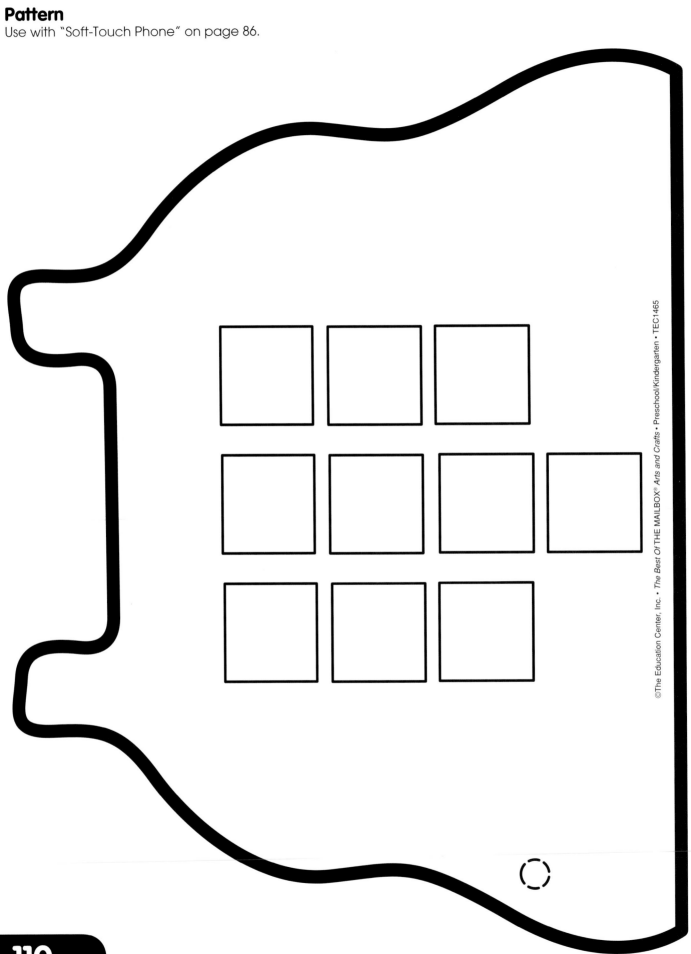

# Index

# Trusted Ideas That Work

## The Best of *The Mailbox*®

One of our most popular best-sellers, *The Best of* The Mailbox®, is a compilation of our subscribers' best teacher-tested ideas. Take advantage of bulletin boards, art activities, centers, and many more creative and practical timesaving ideas. These books have a ton of teaching strategies in store for you! 192 pages.

Supplement your curriculum with
- special units
- literature, writing, & art activities
- bulletin boards
- management tips
- teacher timesavers
- technology ideas

| Preschool/Kindergarten Titles | | Primary Titles | | Intermediate Titles | |
|---|---|---|---|---|---|
| TEC 827. | Preschool | TEC 840. | Primary Book 1 (Grades K–3) | TEC 841. | Intermediate Book 1 (Grades 4–6) |
| TEC 831. | Kindergarten | | | | |
| TEC 844. | Preschool/Kindergarten Book 1 | TEC 845. | Primary Book 2 (Grades 1–3) | TEC 846. | Intermediate Book 2 (Grades 4–6) |
| TEC 892. | Preschool/Kindergarten Book 2 | TEC 838. | Primary Book 3 (Grades 1–3) | TEC 835. | Intermediate Book 3 (Grades 4–6) |

THE BEST OF **The MAILBOX®** Magazine

# Arts and Crafts

Get a fresh supply of fun and educational arts-and-crafts activities with this collection of ideas! The activities included were carefully chosen from *The Preschool Mailbox®* and *The Kindergarten Mailbox®* magazines and compiled into one convenient book. Season by season you'll find easy-to-do, timesaving projects sure to capture your students' interest and unleash their imaginations.

## Here are just some of the many projects you'll find in this resource:

- Fall Foliage Mobile
- Milk-Jug Jack-o'-Lanterns
- Fingerprint Turkeys
- Marvelous Matching Mittens
- "Scent-sational" Gingerbread Folk
- A Valentine Card With Heart

- Gifts Galore for Mom and Dad
- Handprint Sunflowers
- Fourth of July Fun
- Happy Birthday Ideas
- Spaghetti Art
- Plus Plenty of Patterns!

## Also available:

The Education Center®

www.themailbox.com

ISBN 1-56234-323-8

7 21202 01465 6